Also by Merimée Moffitt

Making Little Edens

Free Love Free Fall: Scenes from the West Coast 60s

Berlin Poems and Photographs
(co-authored with Georgia Santa Maria)

NOTES ON SERENITY

AN ABC OF ADDICTION

Dedicated to my loving children, their children, too,
and anyone and everyone affected by addiction

About this book

Poets use forms to capture reluctant poems, words and feelings
floating or buried just out of touch. Villanelles, the ghazal,
pantoums, sonnets, haiku, couplets, slam and hip hop are just
some of the forms used by working poets. The ABCDarien,
though not often credited with historic parentage is sometimes
used to pry images buried deeply or lost somewhere. I had
a student who assured me that ABCDariens, the use of the
alphabet as an organizer and prompt, is an old Hebrew
tradition. Wikipedia says it may be German from the 1600's.
Wherever it hails from, it is in practice in classrooms and
workshops this century, and in this book.

I first met the form in a non-fiction creative writing class when
Pam Houston, author of *Cowboys are My Weakness*, assigned
us to write a story in alphabet form. Each paragraph would
begin with consecutive letters of the alphabet. I wrote about
my son. That may have been the beginning of this alphabet
book. Later, as a teacher, I taught a three-week workshop
on the form and students willingly entered into using the
alphabet as poetic prompts. Consequently, the poems aren't
in chronological order but are oddly alphabetical. Given the
general overarching themes, that makes about as much sense
as any other structure might. Among the poems there are
several ABCDariens, a villanelle, a pantoum, and a ghazal—
at least one of each.

Notes on Serenity
An ABC of Addiction

Poems and Prose
Merimée Moffitt

Merimée Moffitt

For further information contact the author at
merimeemoffitt1@mac.com.

Cover art copyright © 2018 by Amos S. Troxel

ISBN 978-0-692-11788-0

Layout and Design by Bob Sabatini

Merimée Moffitt, Publisher, Albuquerque, NM

Many thanks to Georgia, Jennifer, Tani, the poetry class at Caesar Chavez Community High School, and all the poets and writers who urge me on. Special thanks to my family members who, so far, have let me write about them in poems and stories. Thank you, Randy, for understanding and helping me make my books happen. Thanks to my grandmother who, with her finger wagging in my face, told me "Do something with your life"—I suppose she meant besides all the mothering and working that sometimes can just wait and sometimes can't. Special thanks to all my kids—wow, I owe you for your awesomeness.

Acknowledgments

Some of the poems have been previously published thanks to the following:

Story Circle Network Anthologies "Your Life," and "Car, Tools, Boxes"

Survival: a poets speak anthology "We do what we can" and "Christmas Truce."

The Mas Tequila Review "Janis (Herstory 1967)"

Fixed and Free Anthology "Women Who Worry"

Candle Light Poems in Placitas "Eminent Domain"

Introduction

How can we as a family or we as a nation address the rampant epidemic if we can't speak of it? I became determined not to live in shame, silence, or self-pity over having addiction in the family, an illness without a quick or easy solution. I was three years into Al-Anon before I accepted that I felt sorry for myself for having an addicted child. I learned that my recovery was about me!

As a poet and the mother, sister, child, wife and cousin of countless alcoholics and addicts, I am determined to speak out about addiction and to educate myself in the process. *Notes on Serenity* contains writings loosely linked, presented in the personal, addressed to the universal.

Though the number of families dealing with addiction may be larger than the number who like poetry, mixing the two is my form of creative communication. As I make a poem and work it into something I believe, I uncover my own joy, sorrow, behaviors, beliefs, and defects. I have come to believe in the personal and spiritual aspects of responsibility. The meetings and the writings contribute to my evolution as a human being.

I have also learned facts about big Pharma and the lies perpetuated for profit at the cost of many thousands of American lives. But this book is not an essay on OxyContin or its companion drugs and how they are at the root of much addiction. (Read *Dreamland* by journalist Sam Quiñones.) PBS has covered and recovered the epidemic in their series on the opioid crisis. This book is a look at my own state of mind, my love for my family, and writing my experience, strength and hope.

I believe the twelve step programs have a lot to offer those who suffer, as do counseling and group therapy and supportive family and friends who learn to tend to their own problems and to offer unconditional love.

I also believe that community caring will bring compassionate therapy more often into the discussion. Compassion is the new keyword in forward-thinking treatment for addiction illness. See *Heroin(e)*, a short film nominated for an Oscar 2018. The silence and taboos, the stigma, and the attitude toward those with addiction illness as if they were modern day lepers must stop. The road to recovery can and should be made more available to all, and it is a family disease. If one person has it, the effects ripple through the family like fat bullets. As a nation, we need to help each other, not castigate and moralize.

This collection has helped me cope and love and recover (an on-going process). I am happy to share my story with any families caught in the web of loss that addiction creates. Gratefully, my son has allowed me to publish one piece from his recovery journal. At the time he read his essay to me, he hadn't read my collection of poems. I thought the piece was a perfect way to end the book, giving hope and some knowledge of his recovery.

Contents:

Notes on Serenity
An ABC of Addiction

Autumn, Winter

The kind of love where you feel no pain
a this is it, a lack of concern, youthful bliss
The kind where regrets don't enter
The Dalai Lama kindness kind,
a whole day of glorious weather
You don't criticize, hurt, or want to hurt
The kind where you do no harm
You reduce harm, forge ahead
Where you give yourself a break
knowing the cold will come, the long days.
That kind of love, when you include yourself
in forgiveness, where you forgive weakness
Where dreams are worthy and you put
your energy to work
Where your love is boss and fully employed
When your son smiles with relief
When you forget to weigh yours sins
or his or count successes with a scale
When you love the land like a man,
love the trees and clouds
When you love your spouse, your
friends without jealousy or tally sheets
No little plate you have cooked up
for them to balance in
The kind when you really care and hear
Even vacuuming the rugs is
gratitude for having a rug, a vacuum.
That kind of morning, when
you have opportunities.
That kind of love. That brand new day kind

new dress, good plan, and easy path
kind of day where your body is whole
and dedicated to you being true and your
lover is not the enemy.
That kind of day.

ABCD

An elephant, addiction

like water left on all night
or an elephant in the room.
No certainty, just a
predicament, annoyance

A mother abhors what
hurts her child, fears the hurt
from the elephant's swinging nose

Back and forth: her
steps falter at anger, daunted.
The elephant, also a mother,
stirs the air, scented from lilacs
outside the kitchen window.

Boy in a field, born 1971

a Buddha in rags these days
"I love the wind in the trees," you say
"When I lived with dad," you say,
"I'd lie down in the field."

I see you at eight or nine
an abandoned feeling you told the lady
but not unloved. You said you felt loved
but not wanted. I assess wanting you now.
The bagging looseness covers your strong body,
the boy in the field, speaking, in my kitchen now

Control, cause, cure, cessation

ceaseless cunning
child-like indigence
I, the mother, have the choice
to go or stay
to live or die my way

D

Yes, that. And look, you say,
that giant Dalmation—it's a Great Dane in disguise

Asking for You Made the Difference

The rumpus of food and jackets, yes
survival and the lack of an extra penny;
you were truly my all.
Bikes and mountains our décor.

Pulling up to wait for you at the school in my
old blue truck, you'd open the door
and climb into our little world, a smiling boy
our home the dome on the hill.

Wild rose hips and plums along dirt roads
closer than the missing father.
His forbidden sides of things now are you, missing.
Back then, you and I occupied the summer camp of Taos.

I, through travail to the bone for you, worked
at home and downtown cooking baking sewing for dough
for you my teeth sunk into the sprocket of daily bread.

I pulled up for you, gleaned our honest happiness
from each moment, then stepped forward into the world.
Son, I miss you, wish you'd come by to say hello.

A, B, C, and Basta!

Addict, addict arrested. Addict in after thought.
   Handcuffs in thought bubbles.
Addicted to you, I want your baggy pants free.
All about shelter, compassion, we thrive side by side.
   My mouth learning quiet.
Arrested, your feet stop: orange jumpsuit, hirsute inmates.

After your chaos, quiet kitchens, sane space, sanity reigns.
Another shoe found, another photo.
Another mirror of attitude adjusting addiction.
Abandoment, your slow suicide, squelching spirits.
Around you, we bounce from your madness.
Awful afflictions, illness, my addiction is you.

Bird counting in my yard from the broken blue chair
Beatific, you, as Saint Francis; the birds your companions,
bugs beneath the sun and soil.
Bones aching today,
broken like wedding vows
bending but unknowing, bereavement bitter
belittling when you can't deal, you becoming him
blue-eyed, deep-voiced, smiling him, the father
broken fellow, your father the addict

Chains rattle and I can't control, didn't cause you to
choose no belonging, no cure
cast-off, no cover, no lies from me but silence, you
on the cool adobe tiles you laid, one by one—handy—
cautious speech, the curtain pulled over the past
can't shut out the heartbreak. You are you under the sky.

The Addict's Mom,
an Albuquerque ABCDarian

Amazing how
Breaking Bad my life's become, a
child'choice, a city cutting tin
down the drain doing what
drugs do to a brain, death
each time worse than everyone's loss
Frontier shoot ups too final, too filial
grandpa, grandma, mom, two kids
hurtful as cactus spikes in our eyes
imaginary evidence spreads, intelligent illness
jaded attitudes, prickly pear cushions like
jewels, just say no
killing normalcy
leaving those kids a perforated dad
lacking love, lacking justice,
meth,
nailing a skunk to the gate
no nebulous Shiva clouds, no nuance,
opiated caterpillars smoking hookahs, no
puffy-skirted girls with
polka-dotted shrooms, no
quesadillas with tequila, chi depletion,
queries to no avail
Rough donuts
rolled in sugar-crack circle me
smack, no aid
stupid stupid joke taking him again my
tears of rage chatter timbale fingers, our children

undulate grief's glory, gloomy as Gettysburg
vultures have better manners than those who sneer
What war is this? Our population self-destructing on cue
x'd out for mishap and profit, the crime of
youthful, tender circumstance? As untouched
zealots dance dirty; the zombies dance despair

Addiction

A downpour steady as rain
born first to me, you in a vintage buggy
child myself, your father
centrifugal, flung from us, we
devoted ourselves, baby and I, in Taos light
darling dad-less, daddy's gone
employment holding us in
errant symmetric edges,
flung,
gone from our alluring warmth
his turquoise-eyed deep voice
I followed
junk yard dogs, your father and I,
kind words from him too rough hewn; on
loaned phrases I built a raft,
meager beginnings
mothering alone, warm and safe
nothing from him, he began to delude us
oh the ten dollar check his girlfriend sent
pops, dad, daddy, your papa didn't know
quiet
reigned in us
sitting on the mountainside, the 12 sided-dome, in piñones
skiing your joy when I cooked at the lodge
snow globe world, Taos in the seventies
tears about Jesus who had a dad, why not you, you said
tears, a little boy's, I could only work
three jobs; home for you after school—the bus would drop
    you off
under my joy you played a circus of anxieties
volatile you knew you might choose the gates of Hades to
    seek him

what could I know of the right thing—
wooly-sweatered, down-jacketed, snow paradise falling
    on us
xeriscaped hills under white blankets, sparkling crisp
you, a happy boy
zesty walks to school, joyously you, joyously me.

A baby, my son in the beginning

There were fire works on the 4th (remember Josephine and the M8os?), and Little League (that homerun when Grandpa showed up?) and basketball, frisbie, skateboarding. Randy coached and your baby sisters and I went to every practice and every game. We went camping in the Jemez, sent you to Youth Sports fitness, bought bicycles and roller blades, a skateboard. And still you were so unhappy, so angry. You'd rage at me and I'd rage back. I needed help. Randy needed help. We wound up in first offender's court when you fired a gun in the cemetery with your friends, all holding open beers, at sixteen. Your friend had died, murdered by his own mother. You were grieving. My God, and I, we, had to take that in our stride and keep on trucking. I didn't know, yet, how deep grief can go, but you wouldn't talk. Your dad, the kids in that worst car crash ever, and then that sweet boy Tommy, murdered in his sleep. His mother a real psycho.

I brought you home after you ran away and ran away, but I was so busy being troubled and troublesome; you agreed you wanted to be home. I made beautiful curtains for your room and got you TV and cable. The counselor said, "Don't make him have to earn everything." We were so strapped for cash, easier said than done.

I'd been happy when we lived alone in Taos together for several years, the years you had no dad except a negligent one. Your teacher, the last one when you were with me, said, "He's a happy child. Well liked." I savored those words for life. I wanted to have a decent car and job so you would have a chance when poor hippie had lost its charm for me, and I was working my way to a husband, college, a job. It didn't help that you were six feet tall and looked eighteen in seventh grade.

I was a novice at raising a teenager. Clueless and distracted, not such a great combination. When the vice principal at your middle school suggested skipping you over eighth grade and going directly to ninth, I didn't argue. I had no idea the creep was simply throwing you, my boy, in the trash. Well, it was five weeks into the school year before I got the call that you'd never shown up. You were getting up and pretending to go each morning, showered, dressed nicely. How did I miss the fact that you had no visible books or homework?

The vice-principal at the high school was caustic: "You hippies come down from Taos and expect your kids to conform." I noticed the gang tattoos on this school employee's burly arms: "I'll bet you fifty bucks he's in prison before he's eighteen," in front of you! I had a baby on my arm and the other holding my skirt. I didn't take the bait, not yet knowing my rights and duties. Nor did I shake his hand. I wanted good advice, a program, anything but the snotty assurance that my child was a total waste. It just didn't compute; eventually drugs became visible symptoms of self-medication. These were the early days, just the beginning.

Bless the Holidays

for the day was of the granddaughter
      a day awaited like a baby
for her father had finally texted from
      isolation and denial
for she smiled and told of her friends
      and being hungry we ate
for the love of my husband we
      left him at home
for missing dogs we shed some tears
      admired footgear and old boots too
for her unwrecked car we celebrated, and the
      good luck in her diligent studies
for tree huggers we spoke of deer and bears
      using "irrational" for her parents
for each other, that which is done:
      the uncleaving of those two
for pride she mentioned pies made and
      gratitude for food
for the boyfriend she checked single again
      the boy/man too jealous to trust her
for him she expressed no regrets.
      He was short on partner material.
for her father she gave tears and welcome
      not able to fix the past

The blues got a piece of me

His smile today, my grandson's,
almost thirteen tender, often
seeing the joke,
his smile—I had a fiver for him
tucked in my yellow-flowered oilcloth
purse-ette
his smile bending down to goodbye me
as I dropped him at a red light
his smile at
finding a way even without the dough
to hang out on Central at the yogurt shop
an hour without his
mother or troubled father but with
a friend; his sister would fetch him
that day, early fall bliss, New Mexico
that smile so worth five bucks
in his happy hand,
his other holding Galaxy Samsung,
his soccer ball in his elbow crook'd,
pounds and pounds of school books not for
today because we'd worked our brains
into raisins on proportions,
equations, and solutions, the calisthenics
of mental in my living room
and today, this glorious Friday of today,
he was turned loose to be almost
thirteen without an adult, without the hurriedness
of everything the parents battle
without his grandmother weary, ok
to hang with his friends and him-
self alive and the much deserved fiver would buy
time in the coolest yogurt shop
with nothing to do but enjoy until
his rock-climbing sister picks him up.

a bad case of have to's

the girl astonishes me—so young
creamy skin, innocent hair

still alive on last check. Sweet
gorditos sit with grandmas

abuelitos, fathers, brothers
mamas cry and tell, the stories

the stories that won't end, sprinkled
with jail, death, rehabs and hope

the Gov signs for the facility
a good thing

for male youth, 18—25, a live-in
for survival

more hope. Vans comb the streets
but addicts are often invisible

looking just like our kids and yours,
cute, with easy smiles, curly headed

inside a house with drugs
punching needles, smoking meth

whatever it is, we want them
to stop but only we

can stop only our own raging, fearing
embarrassment, fearing the reaper

only we can change inside
our selves, not theirs

they get so tired of our despair
anger has no place

so stop it. Mind your own tone
your demeanor

Swath yourself in compassion,
like a gas mask, yours first. Be happy.

Buddha Said

Buddha's mom was inconsolable, her son
down by the river under a tree all day
All night seeking the inner light
dancing girls, fruits hidden in their skirts
distracting him.

Scandalous! A prince! Her grief like bulls as
belled cows in Bodi shade warm him
One day he sat up satisfied: The light!
Back home he took to sewing bells on shirts.

His mother cooked and set a table
Grand feasts for all, figurines in clay
gaily portrayed his path, a better plight.
Bright ribbons, jewels, serenity assured
Each soul: Buddha said.

Big Rains, Big Floods

I snap the seat of the Tundra back
to think outside the truck, to look up and watch
the tree shimmy like Aspen or silver Birch
and it's dry. It's droughted but the rain will help.
This deluge bigger than any in my forty
New Mexican years.

There was that flood in Eureka,
when Daddy couldn't get home on time, flights
and cars stranded, then later,
I'd see them hanging in trees
cars or bits of houses, sheds,
dangling half-way up Giant Sequoias
Now that was torrential. I try to
imagine nothing smashing us or flinging us
the time before we knew about AIDS and
addiction.

Chant

pretty fruitless, fruitless tree, fruitless day
waiting for serenity to drop by, to arrive
fedX or UPS to wake me up and say "This is it"
Promise me to chant my glories
anywhere I go, the voice would say
oh wonderful, oh beautiful, child of man & woman
this is your day, your perfect living, snowy
winter day

Cabin Poem, New Mexico, 1970

Daddy didn't understand the cabin—
why I lived there for a year.
My response: "I'm slaying dragons," didn't
mean the little bear on the hill or the 47 below
or the meat we were given by hunters and farmers.
Living renegade in Vallecitos wasn't
the dragon, but the cities I'd fled, my crazy
family instilling no values but thin women
as looking glasses for men,
mother's never-sustained pleasure
on the skewer of Daddy's
condescension—I slayed her harsh ways
in the spatial compartments of memory,
replaced them with early sunsets on darkening
purple horizons of the Ortega Mountains,
with the rising sun's trick high behind the cabin,
bringing long shadows to the valley floor and
morning's excitement of frozen glitter,
pastures plowed before the Gold Rush of coastal history
before the women in big hats sat in electric cars
before John Deere put oxen out of business.
In Vallecitos, the horses and oxen still
pulled iron teeth that tore up soil.
In Vallecitos, it was understood life was brisk,
vivid, and worth living. The dragons
had names like Apathy, Boredom, Confusion
the unsustainable image of Nothing
as a woman's rightful position.
I watched how the elders empowered
and protected each other. How they
guessed wrong about my integrity, accepting my
assertion of selfhood without question.

Christmas Truce

Overall, be kind. Don't tell me
you don't know what kindness is.
The German and British soldiers
lay their weapons down,
took up cigars, played cards and soccer.
Some had whiskey, all had orders for
a truce, Christmas, 1914,
next day, to resume the war
the job they were paid for.

Kindness in that deal.
In Vietnam, the troops took up heroin
and most, upon return, could lay it down.
Some healed themselves in the warmth of
Grandma's allowances or a wife's desire.
Maybe.

I lay fear and worry down, tonight,
and bursts of anger,
like hair combs placed into the
cosmetics bag.

It is human to remember and forget in endless cycles.
It is a kindness to remember that I
control so little, all I can control is me.
If it's a kindness to bite my tongue, so be it.
If it's a kindness to listen, let it happen. If my mouth
has a kindness to share, then share. Do no harm.
We are deputized doctors in the arena of addiction.
Kindness is the only tool, the only medication,
the only recommended intervention.

Car, Tools, Boxes

Car

It's the car sitting in our driveway. The trunk weighed down with extra parts like a lowrider, unlocked; the black leather interior has burly wood details on armrests, the console, a creamy-rich smell. I torment myself about having it junked. Yesterday, I put my finger in the empty keyhole. Tinted windows make it dark inside and out. The presidential model Beamer, bulletproof windows. His car. Up on blocks, his fancy hubs and tires were stolen that night and he cried. Never touched the car again or said a real goodbye. The engine runs; I witnessed the purr. His extra dough not enough for the trannie. He's gone. Down the rabbit hole filled like those empty mine shafts. Toxic grief: drowning in it, I snap awake. Anger is better. I can pull anger together like silly putty, or apart to make blue weapons, but the grief is liquid and way bigger than me or him or his kids. I have given him six days, as long as it took God to make the world. Six days to get the damned heap out of my driveway. It's broken, he's broken, everyone is broken.

Tools

Arranged like jewels heaped in little steel drawers, tidy cases: needle noses, cutters and claws, grips and wrenches, heavy metal. My sign says, "Hands off! This property protected by angels." I am his angel but I'm not. I carried, set-straight, cleaned, fed, you know, but I can't find a damn angel today. Up to him, the last thing the angels said. "All up to him." But they're in me. My eyes and hair, everything, my clothes, shopping lists, the soups and salads. Why do I forget and expect them in front of me like jinn, awaiting my wish? Their feathers, long, black, powerful wings, even they are inside me, so old school. I keep thinking I want drugs, too, but I've tried everything.

I climb in, cozy up for the long haul, the ride out of this particular hell, opposite the rabbit hole, a mirrored image high above it all, a carnival juggernaut and it's just me, being me.

Boxes

His stuff inside, what's left of his stuff, lines the walls of my too-large home. The home my other kids arrive to: visit, sleep, work, play foursquare, shoot baskets, Frisbee in the street, night Frisbee, hot tub soak, club, eat out, catch quick rides to the airport. "Bye Mom, I love you," a sweet memory. 'Cept for him. He is boxes along the wall we ignore. Bathroom stuff, belts, hats, hardhat, photos. Maybe I'll unpack as if box-cutting my veins. Oh sad to let him go like pulling the plug– cut the cord for God's sake. My parents never kept a thing of mine, not even me. All new territory this holding on tight, tight, tight like the third woman on a whirligig. Centrifugal, no, I won't, I can't.

Cotton Candy

There's always an angel of the iPhone
showing the time: Now or Vintage.
Orange alerts slow you down
remind you who stands in your feet.

Showing you the time: Now or Vintage
you often want to return, go back to a place
reminding you of your own sturdy feet, that
glorious dizzy life in the moment.

You often want to go back to that place
a cup of tea enough of a plan.
Your dizzy unfocused life, in the moment
You danced in your own skin, all you had.

A cup of tea measured the future,
life in the slow lane, the silk skirt swirling.
You danced in your own skin, no one owned you.
It's tempting to relax, stop there, just be.

It was life in the slow lane, swirling skirts
orange alerts to slow us down.
It's tempting to relax. Stop there, just be.
There's always the Angel of the iPhone.

The Dummy's Guide to Addiction

Set my default to the Dalai Lama
Wear the Don't Be Mean to Yourself
tee shirt

Have a day of no complaining
A day of worry-free
A day of skipping anything, anywhere

If I've lost a next of kin to drugs
or booze, I'll accept the grief, celebrate
the desert's Morning Glories, the
blue-flowered vine or ecstatic
Hollyhock within my touch

No over, under, or past it;
the gifts are daily.
Daisy chains and love me nots,
a summer day or the foul cold.
It's not: it's not my fault.

Do's n don'ts: note to self

Don't wake up thinking to fix
the cord from my belly to his
severed 44 years ago.
No wonder they ate placentas.

Don't wake up so curious about him.
He's always been private,

sometimes rude when I knock at the door.
Note to self: Remember my facts, and numbers

ecstasies and pleasantries, dining
al fresco by the overgrown wisteria.

Don't say you can't eat if you can't feed him too.
I am not a fixing machine.

This fine summer morning, the pantry
is full of gleaming jars just canned.

The markets overflow, ready to serve;
His bad decisions slam like a door closing on me.

Do be the grandma with popscicles on sick days,
a ride to give; do find my own ideas.

Send them in a letter to my dead parents;
send them to my other children.

He can't see me, even though his eyes see
microscopic bugs, the tiniest birds. Let him be.

Dash of Dalai

The large broken man on the street
collapsed off his bike, half on the white sidewalk.

The doctor walking along stayed until family arrived,
ambulance and suspected broken ribs, and now a missing spleen.

The mom and dad took him home as he had no other place.
"Homeless" his mom told the Trauma nurse, after near death
   for days.

Post-surgery, he hobbles around, his spirits up and down,
   can't bend,
38 staples outside the belly, unmendable between him and
   his wife.

More than half their lives married, two lovely kids
he with no job, business gone, done in by the price of addiction.

He grieves all losses and this: he polishes brass knuckles,
his mom feeds him, hopes the drug detox won't be a problem.

On her porch, he looks thru the apricot tree, mountains
   dusted with snow,
spring in New Mexico. He sharpens his titanium knives.

Everyday is beautiful. He said at dinner he was glad to be alive,
eating his eggs and rice, the mac and cheese she'd made
   from scratch,

her homegrown greens.
As soon as he healed, he was gone.

damn those two horrible years

Oh, I forgot to tell you "No."
I forgot to be the adult
holding you back from his crater
of loss, his slippery skin.
I forgot to be karma, to act karma.
I said, "Do not come back from him a different child."
How idiotic to tell you not to grow in his presence.
You became a windblown tree listing toward hell.
You became Job and I a Pillar of Salt.
You lay yourself down in lonely fields looking for
your lost dog, soaked in motherless-ness
for him; he never had a mom
or dad, your lost-boy father every Wendy loved.

What karma made him choose
me as a mother laboring for him—
a set-up for rebellion— no one could hold him,
everything disappearing except the school bus.
You say you learned to forgive him
but can you forgive me?
Can I?

Dereliction

Yes, that's it: the famous dereliction of duty. Achilles
sulking in his tent, a being of vulnerable immortality.

Men once famous for jumping trains in the Depression
look for work while running from the lack of it. See the
    photos.

Derelicts gather sticks in misty mornings along the Coast.
Campfires forbidden, unsafe heat in droughted mountains.

Kmart and Walmart house big rigs free; cars house
fallen vets who stare into rivers of their own blood flowing.

Fern fronds leap from the mountainside into sun, heralding
sprays of raspberry-colored blooms and trumpeting yellow
    daisies.

Don't stay sad, I tell myself. Rejoice in the effects of choices
    past.
Air, like water, can work its way through rock.

Detox in A Shithouse County Jail
(haikus)

Smashed face feelings hurt
Special Agents lied to me
Inedible food

I don't belong here
Everyone here's an addict
not a criminal

Inhumane fuckers
Take our freedom but torture
Starving freezing hell?

The system sucks, man
Judges own shares, unfair this
broken down black hole

Tense in here tonight
They let half the guards go home
Jail's gone belly up

Two fights in the pod
Twenty minutes without guards
It's scary, Mom

No bail set, illegal—
No doc, cold turkey detox
Not even aspirin

Lay me hard on concrete
My face in concave relief
Are you kidding me?

Expecting Him Home
In Some Kind of Recovery

I resorted to hippie-ism and all that
morning I baked bread.
The dough puffed up like a big pliant sponge,
alive and rising in the warm kitchen sun.

I let my hands guide me through shaping loaves
then rolling out and up into crescents,
sprinkled and smeared with butter
sugar and raisins, sliced thick,
laid loosely in buttered pans;
they baked to a worthy product,
doubled again in size and lightly browned.

When cooled, the glaze would be drizzled
into ribboned hieroglyphics, the DNA-looped
swirls of mother love.
Secret messages from ancient bakers
coded the delicate rolls.

The scent of their baking filled the house for
hours and hours. When he arrived, my little dog and I
cried; and he, happy to be so missed, commented
on how good it smelled. Both of us dismissed
the memories that might have haunted us, the times when
the dog did not do flips of joy, when
I had nothing beautiful I could do or say.

Eminent Domain

Thick cream and something sweet
the coffee ground and percolated

the chair by the wood stove turned
to the window he'd set in decades ago

his fields green and rolling with alfalfa
her garden fenced with crops drooping

tomatoes and corn, onions, scallions,
long-stemmed marigolds and rosemary,

potatoes, eggplants the neighbors brought
the seeds for, squashes and greens.

The doctor said no coffee, no
cigars so he waited then gave in to

his reward for the toil and days of
wind when she wasn't happy but achey,

their collected bones aching together
but she suffered more, not having the cigar.

Her joy was the neighbor's visit when baskets
would come out and trading begin, then cards,

a cake she'd tucked away, or fruit pie, raspberry
from her patch. On lonely days the howling

would make the house clack and she would sew,
or spin, tat, knit, weave—all those woman things.

No that didn't happen. The children needed
school so they left the farm. He worked with iron

she sold eggs, painted skulls, and made fancy dresses
for women whose men smoked in special rooms.

The heart attacks would come,
and all would be lost. No, not true.

They lived long and happy until the coffee
and the cigars were forbidden. Then she

married the rancher from Texas; the place put
dust in her mouth until he died, too, and she

held off the pipeline workers with her
shotgun straight at their frightened faces.

The courts took the corner land with the creek
and brushy woods, so she put the house up for sale with

plans to move to Paris. At least for a while
she'd be served good coffee and ride the trains.

Enviro ghazal, addiction to oil

Sameness drives me mad but he, he thrives on it.
For me? the curvy allure of a well-put phrase, I thrive on it.

Too many calls, I ignore my schedules—
worry tapes like old reel to reels play "I survive on it"

Be here now, the guru says, in the moment,
This is it. Potheads and yoginnis, revive on it.

The soma of smoke while Rome burns, a violin plays.
The planet shakes us; can we contrive on it?

My brother baked me a Linzer Torte for my birthday;
heads turned as he arrived on a bike, the cake tied on it.

An organic fractal extravaganza, just imagine Earth
with lego-like, electric smart roads, solar to drive on it.

Warm winds, Merimee, clean Earth-dream, water to recycle.
We'll gladly compost nourished bodies when we die on it.

Falling wrong

my morning so malleable
like modeling clay I bought you
fresh for trips, hours to while
away, to get to school, to thrive

not always rushing we lived in a hush
my therapist called it deep freeze
she so sure I'd want to blaze like
women lined up for a package deal
a fancy job and fast car

you prodded me, a tiny thorn in
something, my shoe, my heart;
I feared my life too small for you
and so we bailed to mainstream
flailing to get what I was shy of

shapeliness in homes & machines
mania brushing aside those
early days; I can't regret
the unfolding of this full life
stepping, as we did
right into the thick of it

you trusted yourself to me
then I trusted you to him
my willing release, briefly
we lost our hold
you, dizzy from cold
and hungry lack of truth
my darling son, please forgive
I did not know
how alone those fields and paths

nor why he and I did not create
a strong enough net for you
a safe place you are now
putting together out of
bits and pieces
for your own wide-eyed kids

First Year of Retirement

Tiny squash blossoms bloom in the tomato patch
It's October and warm, October orange,
and once again I wreck a conversation with rage.
I want to stick a shiv between her ribs.
I want to disturb her Republican breathing because
she can't believe in climate change, or health care.
She tells me of football players in pink shoes
to raise awareness of breast cancer and I can't be
impressed—raise awareness?
How kind of them to care about a woman's disease.
I fumble a plea to raise awareness for equality in marriage.
She looks as me as if I'd spit in her eye and the deed is done.
Friendly conversation over, she counters with "Well,
that's going to happen eventually" and I snip back
"Well, maybe they could wear teal to raise awareness
of sexual violence; that's the color isn't it?"
She mentions something about role models for
the young and I try to get back the fun of
watching soccer on an orange and blue Burque afternoon
censor myself   get quiet
My brother refuses food from Republicans now—
terminated with our younger sister
for believing the poor are less deserving
born incompetent and stupid.
She said he'd need his new tarp
when he goes to live in tent city.
Portland has several now for the working poor
homeless and hungry.
These American refugee camps have water delivery,
garbage pick up, port-a-potties
the city's attempt to keep order in shanty town.
I'd still like to shiv this woman sitting by me

for defending The Government's every whim,
women who can't be bothered to vote.
I have an impulse, this desire so uncool, so anti-Buddhist,
so self-righteously wrong
I want to stir their minds by tormenting them
but their feathers don't ruffle,
poured into Republican plaster casts
like Steppford wives.
What did they do with their real selves?
My desire to hurt her isn't rational, and
it's just an exercise in letting go, rise above.
Do Not Judge.

47 below

Erratic dreams take me to Vallecitos in the Ortega Mountains
a left onto the last piñon-laden hill before town, the road
winding down into tight valley, vista perfect; adobe
still slippery as snot in snowmelt or rain
Stepping across the arroyo through fence restrung
the growers' cabin's burned remnants in wild grass
I find the firebox door intact,
a relic from that coldest winter of '71
My heart gasps—we existed, you and I
in the valley of the stunning view from our door
the creek past the sloping pastures
peopled with aspen and birch
heaven in every season

Our landlord, Geronimo left us mostly alone,
came to tend his few cows, made chivalrous passes
enticed me to walk on lakes of ice so I would slip
told me I was all he was lacking in his abundance.
His wife Amalia snubbed me royally
but I had no need for Geronimo
who was 60 then to my 25
I had to wrassle his cousin Fermin
on the back path through the gorge,
the sunny riverbank loaded with rose hips
that sprang between high rocky cliffs
old mining rails on the other side.
He ambushed me but it was easy.
I laughed my no thanks and walked on into town
Vallecitos pop. 100 *ancieños* and half a dozen hippies

I wish the cabin were standing as it stood
the century before we rented it,
that summer our bare feet oiled the heavy floorboards
the bed, our bedroom; the rug, our living room
the stove and shelf, our kitchen; the milk can of water our
source; the buckets, our laundry and bathing tub;
kerosene lamps gave vintage light
at night I'd husk blue corn you brought from San Juan Pueblo,
into polenta, the grain grinder clamped on the Morris chair
all yours: the iron bed, the quilts, my vows of fidelity
the string of chiles which lasted all year

Your complexity attracted me, I in simple cotton clothing
seeking peace and happiness, and I want/loved you.
Only the violence made togetherness inexcusably
impossible..
You buried tenderness beyond recognition,
hid your whereabouts so well.
I didn't know your neighborhoods, your
1950s Oakland, the style, the system—
You wouldn't adore me in any familiar way

I picked up the firebox door, a hefty token,
oxidized and rusty, for the boy child you gave me
for the eons it took to loosen myself from you
as if I were starving and you were my all, my everything in
the only basket I'd ever hang from those *vigas* of my chosen
    life

You didn't want me for a wife; you wanted
contact with the goodness you might have been born to
the scent of parents you never had.
I couldn't possibly be enough for you, child as I was

and bearing your son—oh we loved you from our
    broken perches
whatever safety we could find, whatever comfort came our
    way
and we speak of you almost every time we meet, of you
    the father
who wasn't, the father who couldn't, the man who didn't—
    but we
loved you and that's why you came home to us to die

G is for Goddess

I think goddess is gratitude
    self-affirmation good as pancakes with flaxseed meal
    as good as letting the weight of the world slide, let
    unkind argument switch sides, fight for the good guys
    and women, goddesses all

I will walk now, grateful as I can—don't need a mountain
    a few blocks in the hood, me, a leash, my little brown dog
    children, bowls, gatherings with purpose and result

I think I loved Code Pink so much, not just looking good in pink
    but being part of a few women who spoke loud for peace
    to get Heather Wilson off the public plate. We did that.
    She lost.
    For voting with good results, I am grateful.

G is for Goodbye

In those days arranged like
petals tossed, before Marilyn, and Jimi
and Janis died, before Diane and Barbara
and Chuck, Mark, and John were gone. Those days.
The innocent ones, myself, not knowing
the yes of it
improvised time following weather
following a pulse, improvised
funnily enough on a mountain
alone with my son; we lived in weather
our wood pile alive with an axe and stump
our woodstove airtight held all-night embers
star shows in solitude, in snowfall
without explication
without poems, without man musk
or motes of marriage but waiting as
wrong ones fell or failed the initial ascent
until he became your father
until his strength strengthened mine
until, in those days, leaving the brightest light
the magpies' mad dancing their
noise and our footprints literal in adobe
no path back, none visible in front, in those
days, the blind with love led the blind with love

Garment

All weekend luminous from snow
My breath wants to curl up, tuck myself in.
As a dressmaker is aware of the drape,
the level distance from the floor
balanced, fluid, my mind
prowls for a handhold,
a toe hold to get me up
and accounted for.

Weary of solitude and of speech,
nudged by cranial fire
like a cat burglar in black garments
the luminous light from the fridge
glows a jailhouse irritant.

Love is wobbly
soft as marshmallow stilts
The train ride night flight whistles as if I
really could flee to Sierra Club vistas
mountains and seas distracting
loving mother obsessive fixation
on a missing child.
Mea mea mea culpa mea culpa not my
fault didn't cause cannot cure,

Let the universe illuminate each day.
Take a spoon and tidy the plants,
tend to the animals;
make plans to stay alive.

Good Memory for Us

The new girlfriend's altered the way he dresses,
younger, a bit hipster, some color and slim plaids.
He cares about her. She's tall, confident, and young.
The prejudice, like a homeopathic pill, is small but potent.
I don't take the pill or offer one to him—a simple kindness.
There is division between the rule followers and those
who self-destruct in compliance. Screw them all.

He's working on his daughter's totaled car
resuscitating it for her. Putting himself second,
risking this reserved devotion.
She is getting his attention through the language of mechanics,
his deep voice instructing on tire changing.
He makes his deadlines.
The daughter drives away with a new memory,
new from the nightmare of her parents' raggedy divorce.
He cherishes the gift of her soon adulthood.

Even when he takes his cap off
and his hair is styled, I only smile.
I only make eye contact.
Let him read my inner approval.
Silent, like he's been for two years.
Down the hill, the ball game signals
the national anthem and fireworks.
Another summer day has passed.

How do I talk to my addict son?

Call a zillion times or three? Is three a magic number?
The father, the son, and the holy ghost. Who is the ghost?

Wait at least three weeks or months, or three thousand years.
Breathe in and out. Take hikes; nature is a cure.

Don't solicit; nay, nein, don't wallow in it or stalk or follow.
Get a life to live. He might call to speak and listen.
He might be sober.

He loves me, remember? Remember his birth. I fought for him.
He wishes me well. Sitting in the shabby chic flowered chair,
    tying his shoes,
his face sincere. He says, "I love you, Mom, no matter what."

He did what he had to. Someone has to be the bottom line;
    addicts take the plunge.
They exist, a body of souls bumping against each other in
    the shoals, a school, a brotherhood.

As if an astronaut, he slips away from the mother ship onto
    his given path.
Who can say if he had a choice. Businesses, arrangements
    fail. The normal path,
for him, a bed of nails; his marriage carcinogenic to the soul.

He hits the curb running, seeking, life in the dark,
falling with no timeouts or visits home. He sends a
    phone number,
then forgets to call. At least it's a letter under glass,
like a sailor sending news to a sandy shore.

He lets us know he thinks of us, lamenting his dubious
    choices, or hers.
Who am I to guess what he laments? He's always been of a
    different cloth,
and so we get what we get, a shooting star, a bird at the
    feeder.

We must face our own without blaming him for Jack, as he
    might say.
It's not in his control how we face our own.
I have been blessed with this unusual son, my teacher since
    the get go.

Humboldt County Fog

Daddy fled to seek his fortune
farther north, farther into wet green and grey
Depression not a word yet, except for The Great
and mine wasn't
A girl's drug: the barrel chair, an apple
and a book. My cozy time
Daddy's bookshelves our only toys. Nothing else
followed us up the coast, Grandma came with
a cuckoo clock
babies clung to mom, diapers to pin, bottles,
clothes to spin and dry
Depression offset with books, the apples, the chair
the cookie drawer, cigarette drawer. We could
smoke in public at 14, mama said,
keep the weight down, select our brand.
Depression never mentioned—too selfish, Mama said,
to talk of self, her own self locked-in, water tight.
Chores to be done: charwomen, we scrubbed
doomed for having hips and thighs
doomed by my size Daddy proclaimed
"Your weight's ok
but don't gain an ounce, no more for you," he said.
Done is what you are, at eleven.
Your weight declared your final state

Anorexia friended me, *au natural*
don't eat at all, pretend, swirl cereal in one teaspoon
set in the sink, let mama Think you ate
Everything's ok and you're not fat
Food as a drug from the get go, food as a drug
the apple, the chair, the cookies, the book

Heaven in a Humboldt County fog as Daddy learned
to buy and sell, to head north for the trees; in the fifties
it was natural, women home ironing, cleaning
and Daddies seeking fortunes

Heartbreak Hotel

The good doc says it's a bad choice only in the beginning, after that it's disease. We gather in a church with a screen in the sanctuary—the doc talks to us of mental illness and addiction, how they go together, how empathy is part of the solution, not disgust. How addiction is not a lack of morals. It is an overwhelming disease like cancer. Every addict is ailing; each recovery is unique.

The doctor compares soda (Coke, Pepsi . . .) addiction to substance abuse, Big Gulps, no problem, but a daily dose for many months or years leads to diabetes, an irreversible disease. He compares cigarettes to meth smoking; cigarettes now kill more smokers annually than the sum of casualties from all US wars.

For a while you were down to half a pack a day—a huge soda twice a week, and no meth or smack that I knew of until I did know. Then you were awash again in substances, your habit rising like the waters of Katrina. I tell your thirteen-year-old son how sick you are when he asks and that we can only hope you make it. He agrees, and gives a Go Team high five.

A diabetic can give up white sugar, white flour, but the damage is done. To run out in the street after a ball—a bad choice—to have a leg amputated, irreversible.

I heard you say to your son, "I will never abandon you." Where are you?

He said in his card to you, "I will love you forever, Dad, no matter what." But the last two times, as you were cascading down the drain, you weren't all that thrilled to see him. Your gaze strayed to some unknown future. No full bodied hug, no lifting and twirling him as if you fed on the joy of each other. You used to feed on the joy of each other; and then you jilted him and his sister.

"I feel like I might never see him again," he said to me, patting his belly very gently, to show me where this truth had come from, as if his guts confirmed the loss of you. You are gone. We are sorry that you've broken bad; you may be a zombie now. Your son is doing poorly in school without you. He needs you fixing his breakfast, but I know, you can't. I get it, sort of.

I helped your ex-wife go through your stuff in her garage; she's moving to a cheaper place. I salvaged some ancient tools that belonged to your dad and put them with the stuff I hold for you.

Last night I dreamt of you as a small machine with no batteries, no power, the cords cut off, something to recycle. The last time you did this, you came back, but I felt there wasn't much left in you for doing it again. If there exists a heavenly hand, I hope you grasp it. Call home, ET, I'm getting too old for this.

H is for His

His step-father calms me
    Don't overreact, he says
    wait and see
Such an onus on the addict to prove
    his step-dad right
    one-ness is the only deal
In this together, just listen and wait
    anger not the seat I choose
    from which to pontificate
Simply this: a first-born son, a man now
    with new-age skills, a jack-of-all-trades
    no onus: His mother a Jill
His step-dad the one in a crowd who
    plays by the rules and loves loves loves
    to win, steps up to the plate
    and bats his son in
I think to the party guests, ok to leave purses
    the addict's not home, and oh
    I don't think, and he claims, too
    he is not a thief, but I stay silent.
    Mom, he says
    I am an addict, not a thief.

If I say "It's a disease"

I'm not opening a gate to
let personal responsibility
wander into green pastures
like cows grazing among dandelions

I love this boy turned man
who stepped from the oft
chosen road so long ago.
Why must I fight for my right
to be happy about his sobriety?

When I say it's a disease, I'm
not saying there's a certain safety from relapse.
I'm saying I'm happy he is joyous
that someone helped him
when he put his hand out for help.

When I say it's a disease,
I don't mean he was born an addict
but that he fell into the pool without knowing
how to swim, and drowning is an illness
that can kill. When he chose to try drugs
they seemed safer and better than drowning.

When I say it's a disease, I mean it's like
drowning and anyone, you or he, might not
get pulled out in time. He didn't mean to go in
over his head wearing steel-toed boots.
It was a mistake to wear those heavy boots and
thick coat and fall into a deep pool.

I Am Grandmother
for Mr. P

I am mother and I am grand
Larger, and I stand
white-haired, wrinkly smiled
an elder
I cook & bake
give rides and grandma pies
grow cherries and apricots outside
I like your stories, raps and McFlurries
dog walks and the dark
our stoppings at the park
I make you birthday cakes
and pick you up, we like
museums and bones and rocks
and I have rules
no clicking in the house
no inciting riots while I cook
I love to make you smoothies:
fruit yogurt honey and milk
I am like you and I like you
and love you all the time
even if there's not much time
I understand

I don't have to stop thinking a little obsessively.

Don't have to know everything about opioids and crises.
Don't have to save him, the no-show brother, or the
    girlfriend; I can't.
Don't have to dress me up or down; don't need to teach
    pronouns;
I didn't have to say much, just a poem. As mother of the
    bride
I was allowed to flit around in lavender lace and dance heavy
bodied, heavenly bodied, for the happiness of it.
For her friends who came ten thousand miles
to dance the wedding dances too.
Her creamy heirloom satin bunched in hand, radiant.
"Not much light, Mom" she had said. "My friends won't
    dance
if there's too much light." I didn't have to fight or be right.
I could flit around in lavender and visit, eat,
sip juice or water. The ping pong table under the trees
lit like an Edward Hopper, and the jocks played on
ignoring the dance they didn't want. And the toasts were
    heartfelt;
her sister's love bursting through the wall of being older,
my husband's rendition of a poem of mine, his perfect toast.
Smiling faces glancing up under the strings of post-sunset
fairy land lights, and I, yes I, the mother of the bride.
I enjoyed her wedding. The whole day of it.
The whole new family of us.
Hard to beat a perfect weather afternoon
an on-into-the-night outdoor wedding like that.

Earlier, the female rain had wet the seats as we
dashed for the shelter. During the pause,
we ran back to hear the vows,
everyone sitting then on wet amphi-theater benches.

But we didn't care.
Things dry so fast. And only just now, just this once,
the bride and the groom would say their crafted
vows, in public with a mic, to each other and to us.

And the rain washed our faces in
baptismal beginnings.
I inhaled every ray of silver light across
the mesa, every hopeful family member,
every word they made aloud and felt
so bravely to each other.

I saw a tiny woman on page one of the *Times*.

A turquoise scarf holds her flowing hair off the sticky resin
    she gathers.
Where are her sons? For the magenta-poppies sunset in
    Myanmar,
a sole reporter treks to see her.
She stands without a man, without a son.
Her hand grips the bag, the other plucks pods to stuff into
    her sack.

Her joyous clothing celebratory on our side of the globe.
As the poppies disrobe, they drip their amber juices.
Stripes on her bag tie tightly to her waist, the colors
of the earth and orange-gold poppies, her open-necked shirt
reveals burnished skin.

Her family used to grow for medicine: stomach aches, accidents,
but they too, have sons smitten to shards of themselves,
laid waste by the needle, the smoke of the resin, powder
    defiling the nose,
love shrinks back to the size of a seed.
The flowers open and propagate medicine that banishes pain.
Grown on hilltops, one packet inside a pillowcase
will feed her family for a year.

The tree-dotted fairy-land rolls to the edge of the earth.
The hills are quiet as men come for bribes pushed into fists.
Trades are made. High stakes for high grade dope from
the Golden Triangle into which our children disappear.
"Heroin," you said, "is the drug I'm afraid of."
And your anger rose and swept you away in a stream. I miss
    your smile.
Your son asks if I've seen you; we are partners in missing you.

Your small notebook sits by the phone.
Neat entries of names, numbers, and debts
You protected us from your compelling
need to use, took your business elsewhere.
You have covered your power with rags,
laid siege to your sanity. The pretty girlfriend,
I hope both of you wake up alive.

I'd like him to call tonight
I'd like him to be serene

I could tell him about his son's basketball team
I could ask him to get me the keys to

the truck he promised for his son's
birthday. I could say how proud I

am of his kids and how his sisters have
gone home from the wedding weekend

how the balloons astonished the kids
from DC, my soon to be step-grandkids

I could tell him there is hope for a move
to rehab soon. That the new trends will

arrive in time. I could tell him he's
taught me that I can't buy him

out of the mess. There's no bail set. He
fell into a trap and I won't be able to pay.

I will leave that all unsaid. I'll let that
settle itself. How I like his current lawyer.

How I wish he would trust her and be respectful.
How I don't believe she is bought off by the Feds.

How sorry I am he's in jail. How I wish the
last 8 years were different but they aren't.

The future is all he can affect. Not the past.
How I hope he gets his clothes if they

release and transport him to rehab. How sad
the shackles are but how uplifting to hear his laugh.

I could tell him he's on his way to survival if he
can laugh in jail, and appreciate his fellow inmates.

How fucked the system is. How harsh and unfair life
can seem. How we don't have to talk if talking

infuriates him. How I won't cough up for an
expensive lawyer. How he has to get clean or why

would I bother giving him everything? I can't
give him money. I'd rather help his son through college.

How he has to stop lying to me, himself, to
everyone. It's not like we don't know. Stop

bullying me. I could tell him he's smart enough
to do anything, and anger is not the only emotion.

I can't really say anything I haven't already said.
I can't call him. No calling in, just calling out.

If he calls out to me I'll answer. I will listen.
I will encourage him to work with his lawyer.

I will tell him "I love you." I especially love him when
he's clean; if he goes right back to using, to use small.

He's in the jailhouse now. I can see the crowds of men
in red scrub pants, red tee shirts. I can remember his
shackles.

How he walked face down shoulders down from the
courtroom.
Hurting enough from his beating or was it the fall?

42 summers ago he rode his first bike down a country hill,
at the bottom he called to me, "How do I stop, Mom?"

"How do I stop?" He figured it out then and he can
figure it out now. I can tell him to call on his angels.

I Can't Gag Myself: a Letter to My Son

Dear Son,

Hearing your voice on my machine is a relief. Leaving your new number is a respite, a gift. So many gifts in that one message: you know I imagine you out in the desert, homeless in your car, slumped over your steering wheel, but I slap that down like squishing a big cockroach. Your message on my ancient machine relieves me for a while, a few days. Remember that machine from when you were nineteen? You're almost 41 now. Wow. Same one, I think, when the nurse called about your tumor, and I had to find you somewhere in Burque—get you in for tests. You almost died. Same machine as when you told me on the street corner you were going to propose to her, get married, have kids, as if, in your dreams, that would save you.

Maybe it will: someone to live for, like you were for me. Thirty-six years ago, I did a full 180 so you could have one clean and sober parent. It's been steady for me, always improvements on the status quo. That can happen clean and sober, but the other way, well, as they say in NA, unh uh. That's it, the loop eternal until change.

Your update is change. Me not dogging you is change. I'm not playing detective; your wife had that double tracker on your phone? She could find you to read riot acts 11, 12 ad infinatum; did you step out of the loop?

I'm sorry she can't help you. That's rough. The two of you locked in a room, could you laugh? Not my business though, just the kids—I'm teaching your son chess and he's catching on fast, battle whoops and all. Next game he'll be white so he starts. I've got some moves to show him. He might beat me if we keep at it, if she let's me have time with him. I made sure your daughter did her Driver's Ed she wanted so bad. I'm getting her one pair of Urban jeans on Friday after we see the chiropractor about her shoulder and tailbone, treatment three—it's working, slowly.

So you're going to New Orleans for your job with hopes for good money, your own place here when you return. Your kids love you, you know, for being available to them for years—just NOT this year or some of the last. You vacated via that addiction. I hope the Suboxone works well enough. And the programs. I do ACA—you too could ACA. Al-anon? You too. You are so much a people pleaser. When you fear her anger, your al-anon shows like a fat lip. I have to MYOB. Nar-anon counsels me to take care of myself first, like the old oxygen mask on the plane. "Parents, adjust your masks first before assisting your children." Same idea. I keep losing and finding, losing and finding my mask. Breathe. Live. Inspire.

Gramps and I talked about storing your over-mortgaged boat and pop-up trailer in the driveway. If you ask, we can do it. You haven't asked yet. Maybe you're leaving it with her, gonna give family life another go. Personally, between me and some of your friends, we hope you two call it quits. But you know all that. We all hope you two have hit bottom. But, we'll see.

Alive is my prayer; I loved your phone message. Thank you, Son. I'm very grateful for that. I hope the world spills open like a cornucopia to pick and choose from the plenty of life, fun things too, one at a time, one day at a time, calmly. Calm and steady, like you said. Like your boat, like you, the Captain. I love you. Mom

Janis and No Justice in Seattle, 1967

Janis wants us in her dressing room
the manager announces
his fro bent to a watch
Diane and I
like good little Goddesses
single file through the back stage halls
follow our men
to hang out with the divine Ms J

I didn't know then
our lead guitar had dated her
no one filled in facts in the now
unless it was music,
old jazzy blues players
influenced tunes and Janis, too,
oh she could croon

Sitting cross-legged on her sofa—a
sofa in her dressing room! one of her
band in classic pose, back against the wall
one knee lifted
long hair and bony
fingers bent to pick

she grinned at me and assessed
my bias-cut dark green velvet dress,
30's vintage, nothing else but
comin-round the corner curves,
and she assessed these too— no shoes, no bra—
panties too costly for a saddhu

Her curls hung down
framing her smile hands her bottle
'round the circle, a couple joints follow
as we inhale and swallow her booze, same air
same room, my friends played her same stage.

lit up enough to ad lib Go Go
figuring our evening gowns would make up
for lack of practice or skills—that was fucking sobering
Janis 10 feet away and I had to writhe and gyrate
the whole damn song stage left,
drunk and silly on Southern Comfort
didn't bother her, she was fine!
Getting high some kind of surprise

Outside, our long-haired
boyfriends getting the bejesus beat from
heads faces bellies; wrists in cuffs
the cops called them loiterers; they
had no paper contract, having played
the opening set to a crowd of thousands on
a handshake and a promise

The next morning at the courthouse, the judge
took the band's pay. A year's probation
for being long-haired and musical
and back-talking guys, innocent! So we passed go
drove on to Vancouver to the first big light show
Gary Ewing doing Andy Warhol's Marilyn
on a sofa on the wall.
I had to fill in for percussion who was late.
No rehearsal but oh well
The Dead just one stage down—there'd been a pub in
the afternoon where gentleman thought I was for sale
sitting on the men's side with my guy friends

At the beach we fell asleep
in the sun until the frothy waves
curled on my toes—time to hit it, back to
stages, then we could go
home to Portland to my funkadelic
pot bellied stove, standing lamp of
silk and glass, my crazy quilted bed again.
One twilight trip in old cars with good friends
Lifetimes ago.

Just Because 2013

I want to tell the world his step-dad calls him a dog whisperer. My dogs adore him, even obey. He lives in our spare room or room-like space we have to walk through. We want him where we can say good morning and goodnight because he uses drugs, really crazy-making stuff, ever since he sort of gave up heroin. Mama's Rehab and Home Cooking just isn't working.

Progress is slow. Justice as rare; I'm not seeing much justice for those with addiction illness, but compassionate programs are popping up; there is light coming through the cracks.

Kicking It

Kenn said, sitting next to me in the booth, "What would you do if your son became a born again Christian?"

"Well, that's extremely unlikely," I said, thinking I sort of knew what he was getting at. One addiction is as bad as another, or worse. Bob chimed in that meth would be his drug of choice if he were allowed to have such a choice. Apparently, he'd chosen his professorship over meth use. We were in the Flying Star having a brunch and poetry reading.

And I'm not afraid of Born Agains, I found myself thinking two days after that coffee date. I was raised with Catholics, atheists, agnostics, onanists, self-haters, gourmet cooks, a library of books; nuns, priests, bootleggers, hat makers, and artists. Piano players, tobacco smokers, gold rush junkies, and business men who binged on whiskey.

No, Born Agains got nothing on the bad attitudes of my family who never used the word love until early cell phone conversations drove a whole generation to saying "I love you" at the end of every call and goodbye.

I heard the guy calling out to me from the Christian house 43 years ago. "Accept Jesus into your life and your troubles are over." They were cute kids in a Christian commune a block from my apartment on a tree-laden street.

"Okay," I said. I was 8 months pregnant and living in a garret in Eugene, Oregon. Things could've been worse, or better, so I said, "Ok, why not?" Inside they had me kneel and repeat to some poster of a fairly white-looking Jesus, whatever the leader guy said to say. Something about allowing Jesus into my heart. Nothing objectionable. When the speech was over, I wasn't expecting instant salvation, lightning bolts, or cotton candy to rain upon me.

"Bye," I said. Gotta go home now," and they hugged me and said come by any time feeling sorry for me as I was so pregnant and all—no daddy in sight, but I never did. I'd just wave and smile, pushing my son in his buggy to and from the store, or the Laundromat. The Christian kids stopped bugging me, and having Jesus in my heart seemed just fine.

So maybe my baby has Jesus in him too, and that Jesus will help him figure out how and why to stop with the substances that keep him apart from his kids, his family, his friends. Come on, Jesus. Kenn is a bit goofy to think Born Agains are as bad off as meth heads or heroin addicts—not even. Not even close. Jesus was addicted to Love; for Him, and for all us Born Agains, Love is the word.

K

there are days when I'm ok, not totes f'd up, K?
when drugs and you do not top the list but for a sec
when I'm almost OK being me
when it's your disease, OK, not mine

when where you are and what you do is yours
when you told me, seriously, to set me free, a catch
and release shiny trout, you're ok in the big bad world
when it's your problem, this killer disease, not mine
and kicking you anywhere is a non-option
when your kids know it too, kissing you hello and goodbye
when the man-fumed scent of you doesn't bring me down
when you are struggling to live in bicycle clothes
all your colors shades of black, white or grey
well, that brown knit jacket, ok
when all of this and we're not tied in knots
when we slide easily through an hour a moment a day
when no one knocks on the door, when no one calls
to make us answer

Lessons

A cardboard box once carrying a refrigerator is
now filled with sunflowers; Fibonacci gloats over
the spiral like Dorothy, red shoes and singing.
Light reaches my eye divided by the speed
of my grandmother's conception.
Grandpa's gold, weighed and crafted
with an amethyst in the Primavera hair
something for Grandma to wear though they had
thousands of miles on steel rails to go.

The Chinamen lined the tracks with seed,
milked the pods, soothed their elegant need,
delicate highs in Ivory pipes,
the direct ratios of smoke rings to children,
of teakwood to pleasure
of Grandpa's first family to his second, were there more?
Did anything add up to make my mother fail
when she, bright star, could have flown, wax wings or no?
Missing: the joie de vivre, its perfect Renoir restorative.
The tilt of a bottle reflects the light touch of Mother's hand,
pretty nails and ruby lips, her own tableaux of discomfort.

Long Sleeves in Summer a Brand New Thing

Fixing cars, riding your bike, a new thing,
long sleeves covering your old tattoos.
Long sleeves in summer a new thing.
You said your boss required long sleeves
on your tattoos while working.
Then your boss wound up in jail.

Your absence from our home absolute—
you took nothing but your phone,
your biking jacket, jeans.
You left caches of tools carefully organized,
a tessellation of your things under our ping pong table,
under your bed, in our family room,
a public room so we could observe you.
Holing up in the basement had been a fail,
our travel trailer a crazy cage;
your crystal ash in the sink, nothing could decompose.
I looked the other way at burns on the bathroom rug,
circles of sticky residue. Called you out on the smoking trays.
Strike two I called that. And still I fed and loved you.
My addiction our shared space and time.
Attended my meetings while you missed yours.

Never little needles but your fixation
with organizing knives and tools,
from big wire cutters to the tiniest, most delicate
jewelry pliars lined up ready for a photo. But no photo.
The tidiness as if tidiness could save you.
"Heroin," you said, "is the drug I'm afraid of."

Likeable

Lunch box, blue shirt, blue hoodie, gloves, long johns, warm coat
your lunch box and thermos metal, like

the erector set buildings you set up with your hands
clean rooms for chips, kitchens in casinos, whole gas stations,

the Marriot, a concession stand at the zoo, the waterpark slide
the metal arms of the crane you directed to the forms

for the foundation of the school where I would teach.
Anything you built was good shelter, a place that wouldn't

fall down, my carpenter husband who can lift even me
You in work shirts and work jeans and boots and belt sometimes

suspenders for your tool belt and pouches. You came to me
finally for the marriage I'd felt coming toward me on that
     school bus

twenty years before we finally wed, both of us easily distracted
both of us excited about the moment. Your Adonis body

yes, I want you and only you nor do I want to share you nor
do I still get up at four to make your lunches you like made

same day, same way, same order, same drinks, even though
the metal boxes have long fallen apart and away, your work boots
replaced by more comfortable shoes, a racquet exchanged for
the tools of the trade. Your direct gaze still clear dark blue lit

up with a laser fine intention; I love your gnarling fingers
your spectacular legs which cramp sometimes, your willingness

to help in every way, each other. There's something sexy
about us living sober, almost kindly, our fourth decade
   together.

Oh my god, the kids, their kids, their successes and
   problems.
The addicts who can break your tender/flinty heart, too.

Mama Juice

"Let go," they scream

This maternal juice just under my skin
an internal jacket I sometimes forget
Mostly I wake in a full mama
shiver and shimmie just to get going.

They say to stay out of your way
to pray for my own recovery
to let you go; your sass when using
tends to keep me in the game
like a shove to have a little fun, get
a little high on chagrin.

I wait to phone again; they say, "Stay close
don't abandon him."
Your anger at me? Like sticking my hand
in fire, a grinder, my beautiful son.

So many miss you, saddened
by the baffle you wear. You have made
a recipe of yourself: slice, simmer, sauté,
forget.

The feeling man, the tender son, joyous dad
so much gone. Fight, my boy,
Stand up and breathe. They say, "Don't try
to fix. Do not help. He must stand alone.

I wonder and wander about.
What does it mean? It's not my nature
to set us apart. I want to know
and you will tell me when you're ready.
That's all I get. That's what my cells want.

My other kids fill in the space with spills
of fantabulous tales yet my skin yearns
for you to include me; my ears to hear you.
Always, don't we? Want what we can't keep?

Mom

The biscuit cutters showed up again
as I knelt to
clean up the shelves.

The little one with wooden pusher painted red,
a cup upside-down to make circular dents
kid-sized biscuits, and the large one
for those hungry men
a singleton from that set long ago.

I've not yet whipped up and rolled out a batch
in a hillside campground nest
midst trees, sunrise, and flowing creek,
nor near the ocean nor raging river.

My husband comments on my delight:
Who else could be so glad for biscuit cutters?

The large with hoop handle and shiny edge
slices right in to puffy billowing dough.

The sole remaining one of three, I marvel at the reflection
memorializing vintage-loving, long-gone friends.

Only this morning did I remember the rest,
brand new, a gift from you, Mom; only you
could have known how stoked I'd be to have three,
nesting, tin biscuit cutters.

Dear Mother, I at times malign you for
an affection you could not show, the touch
that neither of us knew; so you embraced
the art of butter and dough, the 5 o'clock drink
the proper tools of housewifery.

Your adage of capturing any man's heart
by way of gut and bile, intestinal
seduction, so much servitude, of course
a noose; for you, also, it was not truth.

You didn't really capture dad, who didn't
know what he had,
each one of us a cache of cutting tongues.

The tangible remains: pans, a diamond,
the silver serving dish and spoons; what do they

know but the grumble of stuff or gourmet food,
or the press of nesting us all into one?

It's so human of you, to disappear before your things,
leaving us to tinker, to think of you.

Misplaced

I stand abject, devoid of juice, no plans
like a late winter cockroach.

Up and down the steps of defending him
or her, as in his or her addiction or mine.

I see him as a toddler, a small, strong child;
I had no Idea how tight and close to hold him.

My son on loan, a captive I fed, sheltered,
sewed to clothe in handmade shirts.
(Remember the little bears and the Bowler hat?)

Did he have it in his blood?
Apologetic, once grown, his kids were his world.

Then he misplaced them like socks, dallying
each moment to a delay.

If a big boot stepped up to squish me, I'd hardly care.
So wrong not to value what I have, what I can change.

He says he always finds his way back.
He has to be himself on his own,

off the field; barely breathing, all we are
allowed is to observe, to stay close.

Must Be Now

Mourning dove afternoon, juicy
respite from climate angst
mad flutters of heavy bodied birds
chirping, buzzing, humming, thumping

mustering up Mexico's dusty chakras,
country in the lower half of us,
our shared continent, bird crossing free
exotic fruit, papaya-laden ease
those little grass hut palapas

Miguel Angel our sun-bronzed young landlord
explained to me about columns
of ants thick as his arm.
The powder kept in a box on the wall
to circle the house.

Hammocks looping U's in shade
shadowed pallets on the loft
no windows, grass roof, our path to the river

like a gentle ribbon of sugar
winding to the sea, steps down to
golden warm sand, unpeopled to the
wild sea coast
large driftwood sculptures untouched.
All of us naked, tanning in the silence
of birds
then cooking rice and beans on a fire.

Before we left on the bus
over the mountains through Chiapas,
I had the dream of you,
my son, calling me to come home.
Please come home, Momma,
they are going to cut my hair.

Mistakes Mistakes, But You Were No Mistake. To My Son

"Do you want to?" I asked, sitting on the old Oriental rug; he sat facing me from the edge of the bed. I'd finished the crazy quilt with triple layers of batting inside.

He smiled, "Sure," as if we were planning a trip to Española for supplies from our cabin in the Ortegas, a remote valley paradise. A sawmill up the road where he rolled logs off the pile and onto the saw.

We spent one year, no new jeans, just patches. I knit foot sweaters with double pointed sock needles and thick forest-green wool picked up in a dime store in Española or Santa Fe. We shared sitting in the Morris chair he'd brought from Berkeley. The weather, the coldest cold in forever, was 47 below, probably why I got pregnant. Like a function of the winter storm, pleasure suffused with warmth. Somewhere between control and desire; he often turned his back on me.

Way out there and up the mountain, the old adobe town had 100 people; our valley had us and a baby on the way. The old folks in Vallecitos invited me in the first time I walked by. It was June by then, 1970. A bologna sandwich. Stories. Questions. And Willie the egg lady taught me tortillas and gave me her extra mahogany tortilla roller, a conical pyramid her father had made. Willie's chickens lay at thirty below in their adobe hen house tighter than our cabin.

After he got mad that morning, at me, for throwing the coffee pot, for making a demand about water from the river to do the wash, then a mess when he said no, coffee grounds artistically dripping from the chinking over the hand-hewn logs and onto the board floor. I don't remember his words, just his log-rolling strong hands to let me know I had no rights to anger. Then he threw me, and a week later I hitched a ride to the Coast, in Louie's van, having said no to Louie's beloved Harley.

And your father let me go. I wore a salmon colored A-line dress with a black velvet yoke I'd stitched on the treadle. He almost asked me to stay. Followed us to La Madera, but just kept walking into the Mercantile as my heart tightened up, and I knew I'd be playing with Louie only briefly. I might have stayed if he'd asked me that day. Only on his deathbed, did he tell that story, having been so long lost from us.

Hungry you say, and cold, like a concentration camp. At forty-two, you've been three years off the wagon. The gifts he gave you, a little red wagon and addiction illness. You give your son switchblades —How crazy is that? He's twelve and likes to do right, wants no truck with your dark side. Nor do I. But until death do us part, I will not disappear.

Meth

In the cold Catholic hospital, in the unwed mothers' wing
you coughed for hours to get your little
lungs clear and going. I knew you'd make it.
I slept peacefully in recovery from giving birth.

43 years ago, now I wonder where
you are. A truck pulled up in front and I thought "It's him,
he has returned home, again." My husband smiled at me.
And the driver pulled away, no one exited. A wrong address
Wrong house. Wrong truck. I wrenched my eyes back to the
growing boxes we were covering for winter
the greens we'll pick in the cold, for salads, soups, eating fresh
from the box like cows grazing.

Eight years we've had the boxes
three more years than your first stay with us, your falling
    apart time
business gone, family broken, owing friends, accidents
fixed with pills that really cooked your goose. Smashed
    your wagon.
I turn to my own recovery. Wryly address a willingness
    to live
as if you are the world to me. I chose to live for you back then,
now I choose for me. Spinach, chard, kale, daughters,
    another son
grandkids, husband, in-laws, friends, peacefully
not needing to toss ourselves down the well, to aggravate
    Chaos like
you do. Silly son. Chosen one. What a card to draw.
Your bike sits poised for you, your clothes stacked up clean.
I won't ask where you've been. No one needs
a picture of sofas in hell, big TVs and smoking porches.

Your tools under my table in their cases, under the bed
and your couches, tools in the trailers and garage.
I put the pliers you had arranged like a surgeon's tray,
away, your knives hiding out of sight,
or did they disappear with you, as trade
for basic needs, Camels and meth? Oh my dear son
this can't be you, your job notes so neat with names and dates.

If gone, your son might follow you. Return dead or alive.

Notes on Serenity

I collect tips on serenity like seashells from early travels
in the bathroom, a shell full of shells
the garden shells, window shells
Dalai Lama wisdom amounts to letting go the ocean
this place was eons past; it's not coming back today
the ebb switch to everything right—we'd
be stoned in happy land if we could get
things right and straight, saved up
balanced out, in order, under control, in one basket

I napalmed my own sleep and woke up renewed
never mind the burnt trees, the empty river,
sloppy excuses—yesterday's drowning dream still
pulses serenity, and I wrote that letter instead of
dragging each of us through beds of remorse
it was honest, that note about loving you
there was a time I got by on images of birds
how they weren't cold they weren't naked

Not your fault

not to be thought about much
not to be let down over
no expectations mirrored back
not to suffer but to know gratefully
not to own but to enjoy the loan of a son
not yours to control
not to berate but to praise
not to be shy of but to offer a hand
not to carry like a tombstone
not to tout as a burden
not to forget to forgive
not to worry about or do for
not to blame or hurt or insult
not to abandon but to feel for
not to be embarrassed by
not to be ashamed of
not to starve or fear, this is
not too far from parenting a baby
not unlike tending an old parent
not so different from cancer
not to smoke and drink around
not to feel superior to or destroyed by
not your problem to remember the times of joy
not them but you
not you but them
not them
not you but us

O man

Orgasmic puffs
burning stuff to lungs and free
O world I lift you OFF me
like sketched wild flowers
rapidly blooming the page
tokes of superpowers
O tokes of a day off
from being the loser
from the lover of my kids
to one who cares less
Who cares less? Do I?
O marriage vows gone to lies
today I'm the nice person
the greatest parent
who shows, who doesn't blow
a child off like dandelion seeds
dispersed, I disperse myself
O drug that rages from
zero to eighty and back again
I have no time for perfect kids
O who would believe this
of me?

Owning Up

During peace talks with a beloved addict
the elephants in the room are easily enraged:
Addiction Illness, Recovery, Co-dependency.
None of them have an E for Excused saddled on
their broad and tasseled backs;
their tantrums border on
irrational, more than a bit insane.

My house becomes a museum for
power and sway. Today the ellies seem docile,
diligently holding each other's tails;
beware, however, the way they never forget.

We must consider more than we'd like:
where they will sleep, the noise they'll make
how to get them outside without a stampede
or trampling children with a careless move.

They can be harnessed, contained
sent away if you're lucky,
if you're handy with the tonnage
of preponderance.
They can be trained to perform
a jig or dance in their elephantine bliss.

They won't be outshouted or
belittled or denied; don't even try.
Only kindness can lead an elephant outside.
Please, then, send them back to far away.
Lets get on with our lives.

I do prefer a quiet house
without the dung and trumpeting,
the petty bullying of cows and mates,
their progeny initially so innocent and cute.

Old Black Sheep

Twenty years of abandonment then found
brought home by his son, broken, needing everything

I didn't like how he looked at me, but later that summer
meeting him when I dropped off my grandchild,
our grandchild, his arm swung up around my waist
as we went down the driveway together
and the twenty years were forgiven
because they hadn't been intended to hurt.

That night, hips, arms, legs walking as one
(he may have needed support) his dying body
a few years ahead of me, we held our sides together firmly.
All that was allowed, a surprise walk, a chosen walk,
a how I do love you still kind of walk

At least that's what I felt when he put his arm around me
after my eyes had met my son's faint smile in the July
evening driveway. We walked, then, to our separate
cars, our one precious son watching this rare moment.

Practice

Part of my recovery from the tailspin
is to climb off, well, picture myself letting
go of his shoulders, his manly back, to
unloose my fingers' grip with confidence, let him be.
Put my feet to use, use my legs to leave.
What a joyful relief he must feel without me
hanging on, a self-appointed talisman
orchestrating a voodoo beginning, turning point,
and ending, his stories.

Did I remind myself
to get a life? My addiction. I am
so sorry. My own issues: happiness,
crash avoidance. Stay out of his big boy sandbox.

The velvet card and azalea tree last Mother's Day,
"Now I understand Mother's Day."
"Why?" he said. "Because the bad boys come home?"
And I laughed with delight.
Let me live in serenity, able to relish what
he shares. Who am I to dictate his moves?
What clue about Heaven and Earth
life and death? Kindness is the tool
that fits like new soft-leather shoes.
Why keep the ones that hurt and pinch?

Poppies and Poison, an ABC

After you said "Addicted," splayed on the porch chair
before I frog-jumped in, the word washing me of breath
can't cure, thinking frantic no control
drinking's deck of C's applied
every nerve on red alert,
enabling energetic mama rescue
fire engine red feeling—there is no "we"
giving rides, get help, get Help!
hoping not to contribute
I watch the detox ebb and flow,
just like flu, like jukebox sorrow and sleep,
keys, yours, in my pocket, peaceful
let you be, we find brief contentment
minding my business, mine
not yours, nar-anon, al-anon, anon anon
on with projects, pirouetting to give you shelter
past recoveries held aloft
really, I love you, my son
so similar to your addictions, my addiction to you
teenage-like, my anger laid on like fire
underage addicts rebel with expensive killer habits
very much an unknown life, yours, not mine
wish I could walk to Antarctica, free of heavy chain mail
xtra deep bury myself like diamonds hard to dig
yes, they might throw pie or dirt in my face until
zealous as a caring God, you/I/we sort out the changes

Photo of Us

I returned via plane and a Denver bus in '72
to New Mexico—Taos a touchstone
a place all for me—no one in my family for a thousand miles

My father's presence the exception when the gesture of
the annual visit made us a fluttering sub-family
alive like a small bird rescued

There were no petals falling that winter
at the Pueblo, but the snow made us smile
as my brother, whom he had brought along, snapped
    our picture

That moment: my baby, my father, my brother
my baby's papa—all mine like planets to the sun. Everyone
young and vital in front of the thousand-year-old adobe home.

Quiet, Please

If necessary, do not speak except to listen
If necessary, clip your hair for air
If necessary, take blame like custard
on your tongue between less-sweet layers
of lip; take blame like
wafty cotton shirts take blame,
let it blow through you
like wind on hot skin,
dare to let your lover in.
If necessary, follow your hunch:
trust greased feet slide you as
pieces fall into place; let
bus token eyes touch moonlight
quiet as an empty theater seems full;
reach to feel sand and sea,
dust and water,
everything touches something.
If necessary, be quiet, longer,
more, just listen.

remember

butterscotch-breasted hawks quiet my yard
high perched and swivel headed
not a dove or pigeon all day
yet the little dog barks
watching out for the purse thief
who entered my neighbor's house
new folks from California
smokin' mad about the welcome
from our crummy, crime
riddled city. I'm planning on cookies
to soothe the neighbors. Even in the heat
I'll fire up the oven and bake.
Maybe. Or maybe I'll be
unfriendly too; what did they expect?
No earthquakes or tsunamis, few floods
almost no blizzards anymore. I step around
the pile of dove feathers in the road. Roadrunner at work.
My little dog keeps an eye out for anything
that moves.

I remember that purse snatcher who came
into my house, two babies playing in the yard
long ago. When I saw he had my new Italian leather bag
my father had sent, tucked into his
Levi jacket above three buttoned buttons.
I tackled him. A drug addict someone said.
Big baby belly and all
I wouldn't release him til
he threw down my purse.
I am grateful he didn't throw me down the stairs,
or kick my soon-to-be-born baby.
What a silly I was, risking so much.

But this is the West, and I wasn't
taking anymore shit from anyone. It
was a lovely, creamy leather purse
from my pops and no goddamn thief
was going to walk out with it in his
jacket if I could help it.
Shortly after that baby came along, I started
keeping dogs. Who might bite you. I mean it; I
get so tired of just taking it.
ps Do knock before entering.

Small

Quiet in the kitchen corner old-rose chair
the chair funky with flowered-upholstery patches,
Fall New Mexico sun, the birds, even the owl feathers
my nest. What matters is what I have given.

Balloon frenzy settles after the town,
excited, spits out 5,000 viewers.
The kids got together, grandkids
ex-daughter-in-law (she sent out good vibes
they said).

My rule is keep it
small with her, her marriage
a division against me since the get-go
even though my talents included
her wedding dress, the element
of my fingertips in every stitch. Her dress
as picturesque as these especially round clouds.
Panels of lace. Panels of satin.
Her belly full that day. Hopeful. Fruitful.

Goddess clouds puff like her mama belly
like piled whipped cream
bright white on brilliant blue sky.
It's a Saturday of rest and
planning, a wedding, a
forgiveness, blooming a baby already.

Later she asked, "Why didn't you tell me
I was marrying an addict?" as if my words
could stop the tornado, the roiling storm.
I wonder if she kept the wedding dress
when the marriage went naught, kaput,
all belly up.

Sunset

From my window gossamer pink
warm-rubbed belly pink
old lingerie on pale blue satin pink
New Mexico pink
It's gone, this precious day
like the last kindness
or absolute assurance

The dog snores loudly at night
My husband sits in cocoon
reading into eternity.
I feel carefully spun in
wondering what to break, if to break anything
is wise. Break the silence, break the
mood, break out or wait it out.
It will come like a duck clacking
to scurry me along.
We have shelter. We live.

What sways over us, what shakes me so?

See-saw

So damn lonesome like a see-saw very long and the
fulcrum out-of-reach high, the child alone on that seat
knows well as you do that the fall will be hurtful
bone breaking freaky when whoever the hell it
is slips off the other end, already invisible, soon
weightless, gravity will rule and maim him
falling crashing from his out-of-this-world position

You know this and he knows this and what you
want is hours every day when you do not think
these thoughts about the upcoming catastrophe
the staggering failure of counting on anything
you can do to save him, your child, the one so utterly
addicted to bad decisions

Meth creates the walking dead, angry and violent
dangerous in their rage to be free of meth's grip
Blaming loud in backwards time for changes then
jealous of all who are not caught in the crush.
See-saws are obsolete but drugs can take anyone;
totally equal opportunity.

Sober as Silver

We may laugh about the bad stats en Burque:
homelessness, poverty, single moms,
dads gone bad
hungry families, dwi's, median math scores,
dust. Even the cottonwoods
say goodbye to water, the faucets won't run,
jet fuel in my water supply, fracking for gas
and oil, uranium piles under the huge blue sky.
The economic crash not funny, heroin,
humorless heroin plays to royalty in Chimayo
east of the Sanctuario"s magic dirt pile.

On the plaza in Old Town jewelers sit on stoops,
wares laid bare on patterned blankets from tribes
farther north. Stones set in gleaming silver.
But taking our kids from under our thumbs,
this peddling from far Afghanistan and Mexico—
hurts worse than ever. Our children are poisoned
with meth and smack. Just smoke they say,
waiting at the corner; it's a high, not instant death,
and who but the innocent will trust the devil dope?
Who says No with fists up fighting for them?
Breaking Bad employs, entertains; *Better Call Saul*
strings us along. *Sobriety* has yet to be written.

Today 2012

Goodnight dear day
Today I kissed my husband and held him
I ate a Bob's patty melt (oops, onions)
I lamented the hard life of my dear son
I rejoiced in the beauty of spring—
watermelon clouds on metallic blue
pale cool wind on a soccer field
Today I picked up grandson
and son for soccer
We watched the game and the mountain
We watched one human
I have held a grudge against
I am sorry but I could not say hello
Today I addressed my anger as if
it were a return address: Return to sender
is what happens. No one wants a grudge
Today I accept the fleeting seasons of aging:
my silver hair, antique skin
my beauty and joy of living, my sons
and daughters
Today I wrote poems, fed my dogs
Today I wandered around my house
Today I took a walk wanting to be in nature
but I was in the hood, retirement hood, affluenty.
Today my table is the same mess it's been since Christmas.
Today I started to read a friend's book—it's fabulous.
Today I wore an old golf sweater from the sixties
Today my car is dirty, and I called my friend.
Today I wrote emails about poems and a class I'm teaching
    on-line.
Today I researched ghazals.
Today I am sad my son coughs from smoking.

Today is a day to remember that dept chair I hold a
    grudge against.
His hat. His bulbous nose.
Today I miss my brother and sisters.
Today is the day to plan new veggies in the garden.
Today I put off buying straw and starter plants.
Today I am tired because of extra duties.
I love my husband, but not well enough.
Sometimes well enough.
Today was close to well enough.

To my dear son regarding the grandson

12 steps proclaim respites to pain, a guideline of
don't do's and to do's mixing like blood
an escape from your duties no one can undo for you
change inside combusts a desire for life, fatherhood

How can you do what he did? The don'ts ?
Your son is surprised you are doing what was done to you
Change must ooze up from you not be pasted on by us
and you complain about the double pain of father-loss

Your son says you are doing to him what your dad did to you
astonished that his love and need falls on deadened ears
and you complain about the pain of fatherless son-loss
Hard to believe his real love is not enough, real, not pasted on.

Tragedy in Haiku (newest)

Missing my son,
like being water boarded
and frozen alive.

I have to pretend
all's ok so no one
suffers like I do.

An addicted son
is the longest goodbye,
stuck in time, alone.

My son's DNA
stashed like drugs
in my aging joints.

He deserves fruit and air
not a jail with no
human comforts or books.

My drug addict is
afraid of life without parole.
Two fights in one night
20 minutes before guards arrived.

Who cares; no one
wants to know. It's his fault
so many say in the end.
Like AIDS.

Character defects
gleam in my mirror. What is
his is also mine.

I wish we were Swedes, where
Loss of freedom is punishment enough.
No denial of basic needs
such as pale oak Swedish furniture.

Thanksgiving 2015

As if he were one of the kids no one worries about,
maybe just a friend of the family,
(the odd ball who comes on holidays only)
he was welcomed in,
him and his new girlfriend
though she qualifies as woman,
a lovely woman friend,
his live-in lover whom his own
son and daughter have yet to meet.

But after they had come in and
placed their coats on the guest bed
and settled down beyond the introductions,
their plates filled
and many words of gratitude for having them over,
there was the silent rule: "Do not contribute
to the disease."

No need, on this night of gratitude
for uncomfortable questions about health and welfare,
jobs or futures. Just a willingness to enjoy their presence,
so long awaited. Do no harm; the young woman is
(bravely and with confidence)
"meeting the parents."
No one risked tipping the balance,
the level honesty of it,
like the heavy wooden sea saws of old that children loved,
sometimes straddling the middle all alone,
but for giving thanks
we straddled the middle all together.

"who cleaned up the last supper . . .
standing with rags in hand?"
John Amen and Bob Hicok—

today you called and asked for food

"thinking of this man who said thank you"—Bob Hicok

In your voice I remember the happy boy
now the father of children I adore
The funny woman at the store checking our cart out
spoke of a grandmother who hit kids—you and I were shocked
hitting kids with her arm in a cast, re-breaking the wrist
She was eighty; we are sixty and almost forty
Why does time matter—
Death drops by in little stories
The bagger at the co-op said a woman our age
asked to have her clothes and jewels laid out for
friends—then death came for her
I have labored over helping you as I labored over birthing you
Today after we shopped, you said
something I'd said was true: "To focus on gratitude."
You were glad to see your car filled with groceries again
in this snow globe of economic downturn. It's for the kids.
I offered gratitude like a ride I might have given years ago
a lift from here to there, if you're going my way
You and I go the same way—never having lived far apart
Your thank you wasn't easy to accept
The groceries just a distribution of the goods
from one who has to one who needs
There is shame is this country for giving
as if a helping hand up were cheating—
the grandkids have ice cream
and cookies tonight, steaks

cheaper than burger and Honey Nut Cheerios
In Africa it might have been a goat I'd given you,
my only goat or my twentieth goat makes no difference
If one is hungry, we share. It's how it is
What I loved was what you said about gratitude

treatment

Was I scammed? oh yes
your bones-thin face, you and she
two decades with kids, brittle points dueling
aching with disease you wish and want,
and I wish and want a return
not thru thick and thin
not through anything thick as habits
but to a place you've never been.
Today, methadone, tickets from
the dispensary, pricey as
shoes for the family or new tires or
registration for your truck.

Of course she's mad, Rumplestiltskin ripping
her gut until she collides in overdrive
with her own blue bottles and little pills.
You married her family and she, yours, and
I too spiral like a leaf settles
dead, dry, losing color

The clinic clients need their doses.
In their summer blouses or button-downs
they crave portage, liquid or pill, to any shore but this

From a disturbed underworld
they seek, like you
step-down to the kids' birthdays
arcs and miracles
an angelic, fucking break

For now peeling off overcoats of opiates
pockets stuffed with useless broken tea bags,
tokens of sad, we rise assured by Christmas.
You or I or both will give our selves to ourselves.

Unloading (Summer 2012)

You call asking for co-pays, gas money
lunch delivered to your kid
a set of tires, the rent
Mother's Day champagne for your wife.
You call saying your cupboards your fridge are empty
in a little boy voice; I picture
the iPhones you pay for (3), the cable, dish, Netflix
two packs of Camels per day for you two
her wine, your endless opiates.
You say you will repay
sometimes you do, so we, like dogs hearing "cookie"
can hope for a biscuit.
Your face steamed with self-loathing,
rude at your door; I can't forget
your "What do You want?"
your manners so lacking I think of killing you too.
I can see why your sis-in-law beat you in your sleep
You are not amusing when using
funny polite or nice—all gone.
Your thuggie swagger so high school
your kids confused in muscle memory pain.
You remind me now of the worst of him
his posturing when the world was too big
The swelling up of power and aura
so tired, chi so exhausted, the fight long since over.
In rhinestone-studded gym shorts and buff biceps
are you preparing for prison?
My son, my mess of a son, my loving-father son
my proud-dad good-friend son
you have to make it a little further
add warmth to the 40 winters
since you arrived in that dreamless

coldest starry night, into little valley
pastures quiet with cattle
into the old growers' cabin
the jeweled ribbon of river feeding us all.
Firewood, bears, our Walden Pond,
our gift year fooling you
into choosing us for parents.

Update in a Poem While You Await, in Detention, Permission for Rehab.

I.

I'm not sure if I can die of grief. My heart
swells in the night like an incoming tide,
stored during daylight,
not wanting to inconvenience the happy.
The facts at five am sit like ominous onions,
useless as a hand with no arm.

The Feds swept in for a sting then
men at my house looking for you;
I annoyed them with friendly chatter.
Their badges looked like Halloween toys,
flipped out of well-worn leather wallets.
I thought they were plastic
and asked to feel the edges. They knew then
I didn't watch enough TV.
I treated them like children, asked about their
position on addiction illness.
Not knowing you were slated to be collateral
in their ludicrous war on drugs, I wasn't very careful.

Forty years in Federal prison is an unfitting threat;
addiction isn't a crime any more than
liking a sunny day in New Mexico.
They're bullshitting you, our friend the lawyer said.
I know you as a fixer of all
tangible items, my dryer, the concrete patio—
but you haven't fixed your heart or snuffed that craving.
Even in birth, you were reluctant; you didn't want to come
into this world of angst, the card you drew was a Joker.

They want revenge for you not snitching.
I pray to Angels invisible in gossamer,
to give you a boost. Let you be a happy man, a father .
A friend. Let you work on cars, get legal, pay
taxes. What kind of a country, or state, would take your life
for sliding down the hill of addiction illness?
You deserve a doctor and a counselor.
Hope, not sudden or certain death.

2.

In my leather chair with my feet up, old brass
and marble standing lamp, Oriental rug

from a refuge camp, I sit and plink out
words of distress. Heroin from an opium plant,
toxic taker of children and parents.

My son, you have lost so much.
Last night on the phone we both laughed at your
confession that first thing you will do is smoke
a cigarette. So far 40 days without and you sound
clear and strong. Detoxed. You offered that up as a
kindness to me.

What have you done, Johnny too long at the fair,
from tie dye diapers and calico shirts, to being there?
Those raggedy sleeves, your illness and fear.
Where is the light you step into?
I hear the real you, sober, when we talk now.

Your dog Sheba may guide you home again, son.
I thank you for the joy of you in spite
of the war. You are loved.

It was good to hear your friendly
self, thanking the guy who helped you set

down your dinner tray while we talked. 95% of the men
in your pod, you said, non-violent, just addicts needing help.
Not fair, addicts in a pod. They wait and wait for a shot at rehab.
They wait.

3.
The tornado hopped over you out there in Estancia,
ugly squat prison box on wide golden grasses
but the massive cement steel-girded lid was tornado proof
to everyone's dismay. We laughed at the thought of all the
hoping for a god-sent demolition job to release them.
A little holiday from tedium. No open air today.
Lets hope the system cuts you loose. Ask, seek, and
knock on heavenly doors for guidance
back to your kids, to your sanity and health.

Urgency

It is urgent that I
understand everything right now
I've waited too long
stayed
up too late
Ok, let's try this again:
tablecloths (as in natural fibers and
elegant patterns), bowls (stackable, colorful,
pleasing to the eye, vintage or expensive),
shoes (to fit comfortably my 10.5 EE peasant
foot)
underwear (just-so cotton), money (lots),
cars (that go)
friends (who stay). That puts friends at 7th
on the list.
Underneath this logic lies the
usefulness
of exercise, fresh food, and
love of family.
Oh, ok, I remember
It's deep, man

The Vintage Airstream Creaks at Night

I sleep as if a child in a playhouse
The man who plays the boy sleeps near me

This trip is a cruise across a continent of rivers
the Trinity, the Smith, the Klammath
and trees and more and more trees
and seas and lakes and sage

The yogi said we learn to love
by practicing on those close to us
There is nothing else, the splendor of the
beaches and forests
the longing to be home
and this travel trailer that rocks us in the night
like a train or the backseat of a car as we
move again and again from place to place
driving and driven

Vision Visit from the Addict

Last night, my son, you came into my dream—
a version of yourself, the head-down subdued
you, not the nervous pacing man you've been for
years, nor the laughing, bleached-tip,
bad boy-gone-father look.
But you, last night in my dream,
were wearing an old jeans skirt
I'd made a zillion years ago, one of those
hippie, home-made from old jeans jobbies
we'd lay flat and add triangles to
those cold Taos years.

I asked you in the dream if that was the new style,
thug fathers in jeans skirts and you,
head held down, nodded yes.
It was a silent dream on your part.
You were walking slowly with a pack and a stick
coat ends flapping, your body the normal
heavy version, bent like a Samurai
asking for nothing, just being love,
bowing your hatted pate like that,
dropping in to give me comfort.

We are that close.
I might have kissed your head,
but I was busy feeling elated.
Even in your funny clothes,
I was lifted by your power,
by the sight of you, alive.

we do what we can

without a body to bury
without a goodbye
without ashes in the updraft
without roses from the bridge
without a funeral or burial
without an after school snack
without bacon and eggs waiting: dad, dad
without a father over easy
without his tools and smoke
without his smile and laugh
without his eyes or worker's hands
without much hope allowed
without his green gold eyes
without the common sense and old tattoos
without the soft link that breaks the chain
without a key or lock or door
without his love and muscular body
without a phone call or number to call
without his broken promise and his non-ghost
without finality
without tears and talking in the truck
without hugs or lunch
without touch or scent or soccer times
without this rotten drug
without rot and lies
without this fear, this hunch
without the worry that all is good or not good
without the heartache leaking from feet
without knees, soul, and face

we do what we can

When was he last darling?
When was he cute and lovable?

Any time he was clean and his eyes had laughter
I found him adorable.
Judgment misplaced. Who knows what
he's up against? There but for the grace of
God

Anything but crime.
And then there was crime.
And he was on his own, leaving his
children when he split with his wife.
Only a powerful illness could be that Terrible
The opposite of family. It's an illness, I tell them.
Threefold. Not to mention bills don't get paid,
jobs are lost like loose socks, accidents, unpaid debts.
He becomes a persona non grata.
Of course, don't loan him money, dummies—
it's give or don't give, but addicts
don't take out loans. The drug owns them.
Totally, the most greedy bank in the world.

when I see a strange number

I think it might be him. The little
yellow text bubbles confirm. Him asking
me for advice is like me wafting
the cut-out bottom of a soda can
with drugs on it right under his nose.

But this invitation comes in through
my eyes. My lack of excitement
makes me happy. I'm on the way
to my own recovery from addiction
to him, my firstborn, whom I unwittingly tossed
to Rumplestiltskin
as I live happily with my husband.

It's not about him or me, but his kids.
Ah, not really my business.
I advise in blue bubbles to say
everything he wrote in the yellow bubbles
to them and not to predict an outcome.

I say that kids are forgiving and to call
them asap. I calm any elevation in my pulse.
I see his face, feel his sorrow, but doubt
that I have it right. I'm just his mom.
Only he can help himself.
My help doesn't help.

I'm using the text messages, today,
as if intoxicated. The flutter
in my veins is a taste, a tease.
I ignore the triggers and engage.

For him to be a dad again is
my wish—so like wishing an end to war,
greed, disease.
The little black smart phone
sits face down on the old barber's chair
in the corner.
Don't bother me, I tell my phone.
Leave me alone.

when addiction is organic

it is indeed disease
like cancer without keys
self-harm alarms
go off,
we sail to
our own designer place
either way
a lattice blooms

we paint our path
at rest or work
heirloom pendulous
plentiful
with a teacher's voice
I allow default to
Eyes on My Own Plate

Women Who Worry

Scanning like an addict's mind
winds rush the Mojave, inciting fire,
drought; dangling hinges Hollywood dry,
tines of forks ring their silver history.

Women pace, wonder about pulling up roots.
Anasazi women met in dry willow groves,
planned who could go
who would stay to the last.

Today the young practice
self-denial, preparing for famine
Would we leave family again?

The wind is thick like clean-washed hair
wrapping us in arbitrary lines.
We wonder when to move north, what to do?
It's been an eon since migration.

Who's Addicted to What?

At your parent conferences, well-meaning and sincere teachers surrounded me in an all middle-school alert. "He's a good kid," they said. "Just can't turn in his homework. "Decent and polite—smart, gets the concepts, but doesn't play by our rules."

Another day, the foxy, silver-haired principal pulled a pearl-handled knife with a pointy six-inch blade from her deep drawer. She acted like it was the first shiv she'd ever confiscated. I'd never seen it but was not sufficiently horrified. I didn't think you were a killer; you just liked knives.

I had a baby on my lap and a toddler at my knee. None of your issues seemed overly important, but we started checking homework and making you read with us at night, your step-father and you and I in a circle. You did just fine. And then you were six feet tall at the end of sixth grade, a real girl magnet. In seventh grade you told me you'd be smoking pot soon and dropping out. The fight was on. You were mounting the stairs to our porch and turned calmly to me one morning, saying, "I'm going to and you won't be able to stop me." Well, it turned out you were right.

Mostly it was my temper where I failed, failed to see my mother's rages getting passed along. You were running the streets of Albuquerque by then. I didn't mean to throw you out. Just asked you to stay with a friend for a night. My failure was not to notice, at the time, your grief. You said, "Why are you doing this to me, Mom?" Maybe that was the day you most needed a hug, some mother love. I didn't stop to really think or even to listen. Raging uses knee-jerk reactions, pent up emotions, and the thinking comes later.

"Just one night," I responded, so furious at you over the doing-dishes fight we'd just had.

Back then, I couldn't see my own part, hear my own voice. My frustrations kept washing over us like tsunamis, staining you blue. I can still see you in that small bedroom with the built-in desk, bent over, upset, feeling rejected.

I'd had therapy when you were five or six. My friend reminded me you needed me, your only participating parent. I had to live for you. You had lived for me—I owed you one. Looking back now, I see how many times you saved my ass, even my life, by upsetting me and forcing me to consider stuff I'd prefer not to think about.

In the rages I dished out, I'd fail to be aware and make aware to you how very precious you are to me. I had little idea of how to say so, how to hug, how not to scare you. I hadn't yet learned to be what I really believed in.

I sold my Riverside edition of Shakespeare one day so you could see Joan Jet. I let you earn precious dollars from housework for me that you could spend on concert tickets. You subbed work out to your dark-jacketed, be-chained friends. Some of them shaved their heads, some had six inch, fin-clacking Mohawks, Doc Martins, skinny jeans, and red suspenders. That look, but you all were cute, polite, multi-racial, and helpful. You learned about subbing out jobs.

And then it was fighting about school. You said you were dropping out and you did, like water through our fingers: slippery and unstoppable. The police would do nothing about status offenders back then; you chose early independence.

My 12-stepping started with your first rehab. "You don't have to attend every fight you're invited to" they used to say. Within weeks of starting, I knew why I was in meetings and therapy; not your choices I had to get honest about, but mine (myob).

I announced this to your sisters, then none of them could entice me into a shouting match, or a rage, or a slough of self-pity. I had turned to taking responsibility for my own mouth, feelings, and behaviors. I can thank you for getting me into recovery, and myself for not failing, eventually, to learn some lessons.

What I've Learned in Fifteen Years of 12-Step Programs; a List to Newly Self-identified Co-Dependants

1. Enabling is me lashing the addict to me. Help isn't help. Stop helping as in micromanaging the addict's life. I can only manage my own life.

2. Bargaining, Enragement, Self-Pity, Blame, may be part of love, but they don't reach or touch the addict or addiction any more than your logic affects the sun, moon, and stars. You are a tiny speck of life and addiction is as big as an ocean.

3. Cause (you, not), Cure (you, can't), Control (you, can't) Contribute (you can but don't mean to or want to).

4. The loved ones are addicted to the addict's addiction. That's right. The loved ones get high by engaging in control attempts, enabling, raging, self-pity etc. regarding the addict's addiction. The loved one can kick his/her addiction if and when she/he chooses. Haha, sorry but true.

5. The addict can't help the loved one kick their habit, just as the loved one cannot help the addict kick their addiction.

6. Kicking my addiction to an addict's addiction is a life-long endeavor. Sometimes it substitutes for my life, leaves me no time to be me, to do what I need/want to do.

7. Any amount of sobriety is progress. I am most happy when I am detached from others' addictions. I have time for my life when I leave theirs to them.

8. I love my life and thank my addicts for the learning opportunities they have provided me.

9. Meditation, gratitude, and staying in touch with my support group is positive and helpful to my serenity and peace of mind.

10. Only I am in charge of my feelings, behavior, and attitude. I can only change my own feelings, behavior, and attitude, not those of others such as the addict. The trick is to figure out, if I am an influence, how to be a good influence. Kindness? Sincere kindness?

11. One does not have to attend every fight to which one is invited. "No," and "No thank you," are short and easy ways to not engage in fighting (however, hard to remember).

12. No amount of fight, bribery, pleading or deprivation can change an addict. Only they can change when and why and how, if they choose to change. Don't bank on it and don't hold your breath.

13. Expectations are disappointments in the making. Avoid any and all expectations of the addict. MYOB is a good, easy-to-remember rule.

14. Don't judge. Addiction is an illness not a moral failure. Treat the addict like a human being you care about. They are not lepers. They may be interested in pleasant interactions with you if you are being pleasant. It's not on them to make you feel better or visa versa.

15. You have all the love you need inside of you. Love (unlike cash) does not diminish when you share it.

16. Happiness is a goal for you to shoot for. Not a competition.

17. Honesty with yourself is key to serenity.

18. There are myriad ways to handle any given situation. Own up to your own choices. Be brave. Dare kindness.

19. You can't own or operate a loved one. Peaceful co-existence is a goal. A loved one is neither a possession nor a nut you can crack and get the good stuff out of.

20. Life is magical. Trust yourself and you own universe. Trust your path.

Bonus Thoughts:
21. Seek solitude and enjoy it. Focus on what you want to develop.

22. Rejoice, rejoice in recovery!!!

X'd by you so hurtful

X'd out to invisible
Your ex-wife not convincible
Your kids irretrievable if
you don't exist with or
for or because of
or around, not x'd by them
Never to the curb, you said.
You, extra terrible with
distress.
Now who's kicking whom
and why? What curb?
What purpose?

Your Life

Your dark journey, my winter gift
Fall Equinox child,
half lives lost and found
easy/hard, lucky/ hexed,
anger like apples falling
rich with nutrients,
simple apricots and bread.
Fall Equinox child,
all in halves I juiced
oranges by the 50 lb sack,
asthma she said you didn't have

Ease and struggle cleared our paths,
Missing your father's presence,
missing your blessings
Oranges by the bushel basket,
I juiced the halves
Our dome top home on the mountain
Undiagnosed, you envied Jesus his big-God dad
I swatted demons then let you go,
my Equinox child
A mountain home, dotted *piñones*,
rent in trade for work
I was granted you, my child

the guru therapist goaded me
Hard for vegetables to parent:
thaw out, she said
Me, yes Me. A frozen vegetable parent!
Your teacher called you a happy child,
well-liked, loving fun
You were granted a child,
a guru's words in my head

Taos light, winter gifts,
thank you world, thank you, Son
Your good teacher named you a happy child,
liked, fun loving
My paradox, forgetting, remembering,
long adobe driveways
Bright light winter gift, thank you,
dark universe, thank you, Son
We both know what time we have,
and then we don't know

I observe my paradox,
loving and forgetting,
looping adobe ribbons
A mother's love like storm,
giving and destroying, reaping change

We both know how little time we have,
and then we don't know
My mother love calm,
then a storm nourishing, destroying
Your easy smile and quick appraisals clear a path
In the dark and light,
our journey, my winter gift

Zealous—The New Science of It

Mothers have the dna of all their babies
stashed in their shoulders and knee joints,
cranial cavities. We can hone in on our kids
under our skin and inside theirs with no color code
the blue of inside blood or the red when it is spilt
staining everything, everywhere.
Longing to unite my dna with his,
hers with her kid—this is colorless.
This is like breath, every breath, every sunrise.
This just is.

Zero Degrees of Certainty

I try to box it up,
lid it and screw tight,
a baggie, a ziplock,
anything to keep some
happiness close. Someone
said Don't bank on this
period of sobriety, as in no
security guards, no mojos
dangling, no prayer or religion
has the power. Like the air around
a fire fly. No one owns it.

Just kindness, that's it.
Yesterday, you put a good
. tire on your daughter's car
in time for her to get to
work three hours away.
You noticed three
missing lug nuts, and she
followed you to Auto Zone.
You, my son, took your time,
on time, to help her.
This is bliss. My bliss.

The groceries I'd bought
were on ice. We shopped
so she'd have food because
I decided I could,
you decided on
shoe shopping for work shoes
as a way to be with her.

At goodbyes in the 103 degree
parking lot, her hugs and kisses—
you waved to me with
two fingers to your lips
a sharp look in your eye as
a thank you, an I love you, and
for all this balm I am blessed.

The Last Page

An excerpt from the notebooks of
Amos Seth Troxel

If only we as youth could have this understanding that we are all just here to learn, to find our own meaning. To find our sense of belonging, that these struggles make us who we are. That if we know no struggle, we have no growth. That if we know sorrow and pain, we can truly understand the gift of love, of joy, of happiness, our sense of belonging. We have only what we can see and understand; we can only belong if we understand difference and indifference. We can only grow if we have experiences and understand that everything in life is a lesson to grow from. That easy and simple teaches very little. That struggle and discontent create striving for growth, striving for life.

For me that striving I am speaking of is part of what I believe to be a spiritual awakening. The striving to live life as humbly as possible, to be open, honest, understanding, forgiving, loving, and without judgment. To live my life not just for myself but to live for those who need me. To learn from all who have something to teach. To teach all who have the willingness to learn. To love those who need love. To let all those who need to love me and care for me in, and to accept their care and love. To push no one away, to be accepting of help. To be willing to grow. To be willing to help others and give all I can give of myself. To love myself for who I am and love others for who they are. To only help others in growth, not to try and change them. To accept that we all have our own paths we must take and, without our paths as individuals, we wouldn't be able to learn our own lessons. We wouldn't be able to grow.

We can only offer guidance, but we can freely give love and support.

For me, these principles and feelings are my understanding of my belonging in this life, my understanding of the meaning of life and even death. I feel as though this meaning, or belonging in my life, is why I am still here, alive, free to live, to love, and be loved. I no longer feel lost or without purpose.

About the Author

Merimee Moffitt was born in 1946 in San Mateo, California, at Mills Hospital, the same place her mother and maternal grandfather came into the world. She first attended Reed College in the 60s, dropped out for 17 years, and returned to school at Las Cruces State, then University of NM to earn both a BA (Phi Beta Kappa) and an MA in creative writing. Her first book, *Making Little Edens* chronicles her path in narrative verse with some flash prose. Her second book, *Free Love, Free Fall*, a memoir, is a finalist in the 2017 AZ/NM book awards. Her third book, *Berlin Poems and Photos* took first place in a communications category, photos with text awarded by NM Press Women. She taught in the public schools, both Community College (CNM) and twelve years teaching writing and reading to grades 8 through 12. She still teaches classes in the community. See her website merimemoffitt.com for updates and blogs.

Made in the USA
Columbia, SC
17 August 2018